ten poems

to change

your life

again and again

also by roger housden

ten poems

to change

your life

again and again

ROGER HOUSDEN

HARMONY BOOKS
NEW YORK

All rights reserved.
Published in the United States by Harmony Books,
an imprint of the Crown Publishing Group,
a division of Random House, Inc., New York.
www.crownpublishing.com

Harmony Books is a registered trademark and the Harmony
Books colophon is a trademark of Random House, Inc.

Library of Congress Cataloging-in-Publication Data
Ten poems to change your life again and again /
[edited by] Roger Housden.
    Includes bibliographical references.
      1. Poetry—Collections.   2. Poetry—Translations
into English.   3. Poetry—History and criticism.
    I. Housden, Roger.   II. Title: Ten poems to change
  your life again and again.
    PN6101.T37   2007
    808.81—dc22   2007038658

ISBN 978-0-307-40519-7

Printed in the United States of America

Series design by Karen Minster

10   9   8   7   6   5   4   3   2   1

First Edition

contents

ten poems

to change

your life

again and again

introduction

You know how one day, one year, you think one way, and then the next day, the next year, another? And neither is wrong, but rather a different perspective in a different time? That's how it has been for me with the Ten Poems series. When *Ten Poems to Last a Lifetime* was published in 2004, I said that it would have to last a lifetime because it would be the last of its kind. That book was the fourth in a series that began in 2001, with *Ten Poems to Change Your Life,* and three years later, I felt that I had done as much as I could with the form of taking ten great poems and writing an essay on each of them, an essay that used the poem itself as a doorway, or a mirror, onto the questions, the thoughts, the feelings, that mattered most to me in my life and that I imagined also mattered for others.

Instead of any academic parsing of the text, I made use of my own life stories and experiences to open and develop the themes in the poems. Since *Ten Poems to Change Your Life* was first published, the series has sold over 200,000 copies, so it seems the thoughts and feelings explored there are not mine alone (always a relief and a joy to a writer, who works in solitude, and, it feels sometimes, in a vacuum) but are living questions and concerns in the hearts and minds of many. The poems, then, and I hope my essays too, gave voice to layers of feelings that many people could respond to. Although readers felt the echoes of the poems in their own lives, they may not have put them into words. It is a privilege to have given voice to people's dreams, aspirations, and questions in this way.

Based on the e-mails I have received, the series has served another purpose, too. It has rekindled a love of poetry in people who may have been inspired by it earlier in their lives but whose days have since become filled with other, more pressing concerns: children, family, career, the mortgage. It has also introduced many people to poetry who otherwise would never have picked up a poetry book. Poetry is intimidating for many of us. It is all too reminiscent of dull classrooms at the end of an already-long day. The language can be daunting, too, especially in the poetry you might remember faintly from college, or in much of the poetry in many anthologies.

The language of the poems I chose for the series was deliberately accessible (which is not necessarily to say simple), and mostly by contemporary poets or by mystical poets, such as Rumi, with contemporary translations. And the essays, it appears, became safe entry points for the reader new to poetry to get her feet wet. Then, as the reader enters into the text with more confidence and curiosity, she can begin to fall under poetry's spell, its rhythms and incantatory magic, which assist in the absorption of the sentiments and perceptions that are voiced there.

This is all by way of introduction to the obvious: that I am now, in June of 2007, sitting at my desk putting the finishing touches on the book you have just opened, yes, *Ten Poems to Change Your Life Again and Again.* My first response to the question of why I have decided to take up this particular theme once more is that my own life has changed dramatically during these last couple of years. So many new horizons have opened up before me, as old ones recede into memory, that I have felt the need for both a mirror of the insights I have been given and also a vehicle within which to explore the different facets of my current life experience. I have also wanted a mirror for my continuing and lifelong exploration of what a spiritual life in this everyday world can look like: what questions it raises, what paradoxes it invites us to resolve. And since I wanted a universal language, rather than that of a specific religious tradition, I could think of no better vehicle for all this than poetry.

Every one of the poems in this book has struck me a blow, a direct hit, each of them, into the heart of hearts. Every one of them, in its own way, has opened a door for me to go deeper into my own experience, my own longings, my own sorrows and joys, and into the silence that surrounds all of this, all of us, always. Through these poems I have been able to unravel the nuances and subtleties of feeling that have flowed from the events of my life. Through the mirror pool of these poems, my life has become clearer, quieter, more trusting. It has become what it was already becoming, but the poems have given me the inspiration to inform the process in language. I have no doubt that, like all great literature, these poems can change a person's life—in a heartbeat.

It's true that on occasion in the last few years, while spending many hours writing books on poetry, I have wondered whether I was wasting my time. After all, the world is in trouble. It has always been in trouble. Surely, there must be something more useful, more pressing, to give my time to than reflecting on poetry? Couldn't I go and start a project in Africa, or at least do some small thing to help prevent climate catastrophe; start reducing my own carbon footprint, for example, and begin a movement to encourage others to do the same? But no; I wrote more poetry books, wondering at times whether they and I were doing little more than making ourselves progressively irrelevant.

I knew better, which is why I kept writing; which is why I reversed my decision and decided to write this book. I know that great poetry has the power to start a fire in a person's life. It can alter the way we see ourselves. It can change the way we see the world. More than anything, a great poem tells us the truth. And it calls us to face the truth in ourselves. This, I believe, more than anything else, is why a great poem can change someone's life.

There is no better way to tell the truth through words than via a poem. In a good poem, every single word matters. It must be the right word, the truest word for what the poet is searching to convey. Poetry is precise speech. I have heard it said that to write, you must love sentences. To write poetry, you must love words and images. The poet is a fisher of words and images. She drops her line down into the deeper waters, below surface impressions, and waits, sometimes a long time. Then there will be a tug on the line and she will reel in the exact right phrase or image to convey the feeling or thought she wants to capture. The thought or the feeling itself must be sifted like grain; she must distinguish the many shades and densities until she knows she has touched the essence of it. It is not enough to generalize, to use well-worn or easy phrases. Poetry deals with the particular—this particular density and shape of feeling, that specific object, this exact sunrise, this morning, this great love. It is the particular that can best open us into the universal.

In this way, poetry calls us to pay attention, to pay attention both to the world around us and also to the world within. Poetry is a way of rescuing the world from oblivion by the practice of attention. It is our attention that honors and gives value to living things, that gives them their proper name and particularity, and retrieves them from the obscurity of the general. It is the same faculty that can distinguish and name the subtle layers in a feeling. When I pay attention, something in me wakes up, and that something is much closer to who I am than the driven or drifting self I usually take myself to be. I am straightened somehow, made truer, brought to a deeper life.

So the poems in this book have encouraged me to be as attentive as I can when pondering their meanings and, in the process, describing the truth of my own experience in the essays. Their rigor and integrity have encouraged me to aspire to a similar standard, to find the words and the sentences that can give the truest shape to the elusive qualities of feeling and perception that have coursed through my own heart and mind. The love, loss, joy, change, and delight in this world you will find in the poems are echoed and brought to ground in the example of my one, particular, breathing human life. My hope is you will find yourself reflected there.

Through even one poem, through the story of even one human being, we ourselves can feel more deeply our relation to others. This is another way in which poetry can be life changing: It can make us more fully human. Jane Hirshfield, one of the poets in this book, has said it this way: "Whether from reading the New England Transcendentalists or Eskimo poetry, I feel that everything I know about being human has been deepened by the poems I've read."[1]

John Keats spoke of this humanizing power too, when he said, "Poetry should strike the reader as a wording of his own highest thoughts, and appear almost as a Remembrance."[2]

The same remembrance is the theme of David Whyte's poem in this book. That's all very well, you might say; poems may be a humanizing influence; they may even carry us to the heights of spiritual insight and realization. But what have they done to shift the world's obsession with power, greed, and violence? What has a poem done to dissolve injustice? This argument has been rising and falling for centuries, but consider this: Poetry and literature in general have been routinely banned around the world at different times because of their subversive influence. If poetry and literature are humanizing influences, they work directly against those regimes and ideologies that restrict rather than encourage liberty and justice. It is probably no coincidence that more books have been translated into Spanish in the last year than have been translated into Arabic in the last five hundred years.

Because it pays such close attention to the particular, poetry generates empathy—empathy for others and for all living things. Through empathy, it connects different worlds, different ideas, and different people and things. When, through a poetic act of imagination, one feels kinship with others and with all life, it is that much more difficult to oppress others. And that, in a tyrannical regime, is subversion.

Stalin tried to strip Russia of its soul with his death camps. Osip Mandelstam restored that soul by reciting poetry to his fellow convicts and by writing about it in his journal. "Perhaps to remain a poet in such circumstances," Saul Bellow wrote, "is also to reach the heart of politics. The human feelings, human experiences, the human form and face, recover their proper place—the foreground."[3]

This is what I feel Jack Gilbert does in his remarkable poem in this volume, "A Brief for the Defense." In questioning our responsibility in the face of the world's suffering, he says,

> *. . . We must have*
> *the stubbornness to accept our gladness in the ruthless*
> *furnace of this world. . . .*

This is a poetic response to the question, a response that does not for a moment replace the need for action in the world, but is equally necessary.

Gilbert's poem is the only one in this book to address directly the sorrows of the world we live in. Leonard Cohen in "Leaving Mt. Baldy" and Marie Howe in "What the Living Do" take as their subject the world of our everyday lives, but from a different perspective. Cohen's poem dissolves any notion we may have that the world of the spirit and this humdrum world we live in are in any sense fundamentally different. Howe plunges us into her daily experience of dropping things, forgetting them, the dishes piling up in the sink, and then suddenly catching sight of herself in the window of the local video store,

> . . . And I'm gripped by a
> cherishing so deep
>
> for my own blowing hair, chapped face, and
>   unbuttoned coat that
> I'm speechless:
> I am living, I remember you.

This is what I mean by poetry arousing empathy. Who does not feel with her, for her, when she spills her coffee down her sleeve, when she drops her bag of groceries, there in the middle of her ordinary life, in which she suddenly sees in a window her own imperfect beauty? Howe's poem can change the way we see our own imperfect, beautiful lives.

Two more poems address in different ways the fact of change. Rainer Maria Rilke's *Sonnets to Orpheus,* Part Two, XII begins with

> Want the change. Be inspired by the flame
> Where everything shines as it disappears.

Rilke's poem is relentless in its insistence that we welcome the passing of things, life's unceasing movement, with one bright image following after another. Jane Hirshfield's "Each Moment a White Bull Steps Shining into the World" encouraged me to mine the depths of my own experience of love. The white bull signifies not just change, but something momentous, entirely unexpected, storming into your life like a wild animal.

Love is also the theme of Ellen Bass's "Gate C22," one of the more luscious and delightful poems I have ever read. And in "Awaken as the Beloved," St. Symeon the Theologian goes further than any Christian I know in identifying himself with God and declaring that we are that, too. Hafiz suggests that we alone are the source of love in "With That Moon Language"; so why not say

what every other eye in this world is dying to hear?

Finally, C. P. Cavafy, the Greek poet, reminds us in his towering poem "Ithaka" that we are the heroes of our own story, and that the journey is everything. Savor it, he says, take your time in foreign ports, there is no rush to get where you are going, since it is inevitable you will get there in the end.

And if you find her poor, Ithaka won't have fooled you.
Wise as you have become, so full of experience,
You'll have understood by then what these Ithakas mean.

My hope is that you will reach the end of this book and will have understood by then, if not before, how poetry can be not only life sustaining, a necessary food, but how in profound if imperceptible ways it can even change the course of human history. There's a headstone in a Long Island graveyard—the one where Jackson Pollock is buried—that I think encapsulates the value and life-giving qualities of poetry in a world in which there are so many sorrows. It says,

ARTISTS AND POETS ARE THE RAW
NERVE ENDS OF HUMANITY.
BY THEMSELVES THEY CAN DO
LITTLE TO SAVE HUMANITY.
WITHOUT THEM THERE WOULD BE
LITTLE WORTH SAVING.

1

SONNETS TO ORPHEUS, PART TWO, XII

by Rainer Maria Rilke

Want the change. Be inspired by the flame
Where everything shines as it disappears.
The artist, when sketching, loves nothing so much
as the curve of the body as it turns away.

What locks itself in sameness has congealed.
Is it safer to be gray and numb?
What turns hard becomes rigid
and is easily shattered.

Pour yourself like a fountain.
Flow into the knowledge that what you are seeking
finishes often at the start, and, with ending, begins.

Every happiness is the child of a separation
it did not think it could survive. And Daphne,
becoming a laurel,
dares you to become the wind.

(translated by Anita Barrows and Joanna Macy)

want the change

This is a beautiful translation of one of the poems in Rilke's last, and many say his greatest, work, *Sonnets to Orpheus*. Certainly, the *Sonnets* have found their rightful place in the canon of great twentieth-century European literature; and this sonnet in particular has found its way into my own heart as a resounding call to new life after the eventual demise of my marriage with Maria, the same Maria I first met in a retreat center in the middle of hay fields. That encounter was described in the original volume of *Ten Poems to Change Your Life*. This sonnet signals for me the other end of the story.

The *Sonnets to Orpheus* came about in a mysterious way. Before the First World War, Rilke had begun work on what he felt would be his most inspired work, the *Duino Elegies*, but during the war he found it increasingly impossible to write, and only in 1921 did he find the peace of mind and also the place where the muse could speak to him again. In that year, funded by wealthy friends, Rilke moved to the thirteenth-century Château de Muzot, in Switzerland. In a seminal moment of serendipity, his lover at the time, Baladine Klossowska, left a postcard pinned above his desk, and then withdrew. It showed Orpheus under a tree with his lyre, singing to the animals.

For months Rilke wrote nothing but correspondence, and a lot of it, until suddenly, early in 1922, a great wave of poetry surged up within him and poured onto the page in the form of a series of sonnets to Orpheus. In just over two weeks, fifty-five poems arrived complete, in the standard sonnet form of fourteen lines with end rhymes. They arrived with an astonishing speed and fluidity that seemed to suggest they had been dictated to him rather than having germinated in his mind. In between the sonnets, he also wrote the seventh, the eighth, the ninth, and the tenth *Duino Elegies,* completing that series as well.

Now Orpheus was a god and a poet, and the sweetness of his voice would cause trees to walk and animals to draw near. When his beloved Eurydice died from a snake bite, he went down into the Underworld and enchanted its ruler, Hades, with his music, persuading him to allow him to return to Earth with Eurydice. Hades agreed on condition that Orpheus not turn to look at his beloved on the journey, though he did, of course, just before reaching the light; otherwise, there would have been no story. His punishment was to be torn to shreds by the Maenads, the female worshippers of Dionysus. They threw his head into the river Hebrus, and it floated, still singing, down to the sea. In this last detail we have the perfect image for Rilke's insistence throughout his work that the poet be a praising person; that whatever his fate, his song is all, and will not perish.

Dismemberment is a theme in every religion—from the ancient Egyptian god Osiris, through the Tibetan meditation practice called *chod* (in which you visualize your own dismemberment), down to the Christian celebration of the Eucharist, "This is my body, broken for you."

In the sacrifice of the idea of the bodily self—the identification of self with form—lies the possibility of transcendence and of a new life. And if there was ever a poet who urged his readers to transform their lives in this way, it was Rilke. One of his best-known poems, the "Archaic Torso of Apollo," even ends with the lines

> *for there is no place at all*
> *that isn't looking at you. You must change your life.*[1]

In the sonnet before us here, he urges the change upon us in the very first line. For change happens in every moment. Not just the events of our lives, but the cells in our bodies, our memories, even our sense of who we are, all shift in a moment, often imperceptibly. We, on the other hand, tend to nurture a fixed idea of who we are and where we are going. We harbor notions of what is good for us and what is not, and try to organize and strategize accordingly.

Yet life does what it does with scant concern for our preferences, so the poet is urging us to look beyond the parade of circumstances and events to the fundamental fact of change itself. In wanting the change, we are aligning ourselves with truth, with what is already happening anyway. We flow, rather than self-consciously make our own way. And in that flow the sense of who we are and where we are going becomes more malleable and fluid, more responsive to conditions around us instead of bound by fixed beliefs and agendas. In the flow of change, self-forgetting happens, and a deeper remembrance can emerge, the remembrance of being always and ever joined to a greater life—not as another idea or elegant concept, but as a lived experience in the moment.

In another translation of this first line, Herter Norton renders it as *Will the transformation*. Not just change from one appearance, one set of contingencies, to another, then, but transformation: a metamorphosis involving a different order, a different quality of being and seeing altogether. Not a horizontal shift from one room in the mind to another, but a vertical ascent into a quality beyond the original mindset altogether. (Is it merely by chance that Rilke spent many hours with Baladine—his lover who pinned the postcard of Orpheus by his desk—reading Ovid's *Metamorphoses*?)

So Rilke is urging us to want the change that is happening, to embrace it, whatever it is. If we are in the middle of a divorce, let it be that; if we have lost our job, let it be that, and if we are dying, may it be so. Of course it's not easy. Nobody willingly allows themselves to be dismembered, torn apart, crushed like a grape between fingers. The ego, our idea of who we think we are, will never assent to self-sacrifice. The impulse must come from something else in us, another organ of awareness, you might say, that knows somehow that, however much it hurts, however much we may be on the rack—a sacrificial lamb, it may seem to us—that what is happening is true, necessary, inevitable, and ultimately, therefore, good.

Easy enough to say, but it didn't quite feel like that for me when, at the beginning of 2006, eight years after first meeting her, I finally parted from my wife, Maria—the same Maria I had met in near-mythic circumstances in what felt like a visitation from destiny. She was a muse for me, and her beauty and thoughtful calm inspired me till the end. Yet there were also deep incompatibilities, which for a while we both let the charisma, the magic of our togetherness, gloss over. But increasingly, over the space of a few years, it became evident that our lives had very different trajectories and priorities.

With hindsight, I can see that the end had been whispered in my ear from the very beginning. A week or two after we had parted ways at the retreat house (Maria to return to her family in New Jersey, and I to a writer's cabin to continue working on a book, with no plans to make contact again), I was awoken early one morning with a start. I would not call this a dream, more of a visitation; three owls were sitting on a branch, all eyes on me. As I stared back at them, they flew one by one in front of me: their hooting filling, it seemed, the entire room. My mind was filled with two words: *Attention! Attention! Warning! Warning!* That same afternoon, Maria e-mailed me for the first time. I didn't even know she had my address, since we had not exchanged any details when leaving the retreat center. I knew this was what the owls were telling me to pay attention to—it was my choice to respond or not, and either way, it would be fateful. I went ahead and responded. Two years later, we were married.

Many things contribute to the end of a marriage, and

there is no need for me to explore them here. Suffice it to say that when the time finally came for our parting, we were both more than ready for it due to our different reasons. But that doesn't mean it was easy, at least for me. It's one thing to know you need to part and start a new life; it's another to say good-bye and close the door on a crucial chapter in your life—*to want the change, to will the transformation.*

For the first time in my life, I was without a significant other to relate to. My three relationships had spanned thirty years, with almost no gap between them. To begin with, being alone was, and still is at times, a strange and sometimes disorienting sensation. Of necessity, my attention was returned to my own life, distinct from anyone else's. I saw how much energy and time I had given to concerning myself with the life of someone else. You might call it codependency, or simply an engagement in the joys and struggles of someone you love. It was probably a mixture of both.

In any event, over time, I have come to value myself as an individual, rather than as part of a couple, in a new way. I had always assumed myself to be well grounded in my own individuality, and in many ways I was. But it is only in the experience of having no external referent, either physical or imaginary, that I have come to feel both a deeper substance and also a deeper tenderness in my own life, which has allowed me to be more porous and open to the mystery of how everything unfolds, than I had before.

Intermittent loneliness, along with the grief of our parting, and the relief of knowing, despite everything, the rightness of it all, would often vie for my attention, as did the knowledge that a new life was beckoning me in California. I had made my first home there after arriving in the United States from England, and I had always felt more at home in that state than on the East Coast (where we had moved to be near Maria's children), with its more somber weather and temperament. The day after I arrived in California, I wept for a long time in the arms of a dear friend, who held me like her child. It was all very humbling, a necessary dismembering, as I see it now to have been.

But the shift, the full surrender to the change that Rilke speaks to in this poem, actually occurred for me some time later, when I read another poem, called "The God Abandons Antony," by C. P. Cavafy. Or perhaps I should say it was articulated then, and was already present, unspoken, within me, waiting for the right words to give it birth. Astonishing poem! Antony and Cleopatra have lost their cherished city of Alexandria. Antony has also lost the protection of his personal god, Dionysus, god of wine and music. The poet commands him to go to the window and listen to the beautiful music of a procession as it passes in the street—to listen, knowing that this is what he is losing. To listen

> *to the exquisite music of that strange procession,*
> *and say goodbye to her, to the Alexandria that you*
> *are losing.*[2]

Reading those lines was like undoing the last button on a tight shirt. A few days later I visited Maria, sat down on the sofa with her, and read her this poem. I wanted her to know that I could feel the richness of what I was losing, that I would not wish to diminish our life together by suggesting she didn't matter to me, that I would always recognize and praise the gifts she had brought into my life. How could I not? And yet we were already gone from each other.

The sadness and yes, sometimes the anger, would surface every now and then for a while after that, but essentially I was released from my own morbid preoccupations into a new life with new possibilities that were far more congruent with my natural inclinations than the life I had known with Maria could ever have allowed. And I know she would say the same.

A year or so later, I returned to New York for a friend's book party. There she was, and we fell into each other's arms, though only for two minutes—that was enough for us both to know the love hadn't gone anywhere, even though our lives were now on very different tracks and in different time zones, with no regrets.

This is exactly what it felt like when I first read this image in Rilke's poem:

> *. . . Be inspired by the flame*
> *Where everything shines as it disappears.*

This awakens in me the same clarity and sense of joy that I felt on reading Cavafy's lines. The love and the life I knew with Maria were never so bright as when I could fully acknowledge their leaving. It's like death in a way, the proximity of which can sharpen our vision and deepen our gratitude. A friend just told me that he has known for the last two weeks that he has prostate cancer. These two weeks, he said, have been the most alive in his life. Far from feeling fear or grief (perhaps these are still to come), every moment has had a clarity and sharpness he has hardly ever known. It's as if some deeper vision has been switched on, which enables him to see with great intensity the fullness of each moment.

I find the next image, owing as much to the translators as to Rilke, one of the most beautiful of all.

> *The artist, when sketching, loves nothing so much*
> *as the curve of the body as it turns away.*

This image has made me appreciate with completely fresh eyes those nude figures turning away from the viewer that you can see in the work of so many artists throughout history, from Roman times to Picasso. It's not just a matter of perspective, but of the interplay of absence and presence, of an eye that can flow into the future even as it is happening in .the present.

The next stanza warns us that the more we cling to a form, whether it be the form of a relationship, a career, or a belief system, the more prone we are to earthquakes and lightning bolts. The more hard and rigid something is, the more susceptible it is to the forces of change, both within and without. And since change is life, change will keep coming right up until the final big change. Which is why it is better, rather than protecting ourselves with some false sense of detachment, to allow what is happening, to flow with it like water, another life image.

> *Flow into the knowledge that what you are seeking*
> *finishes often at the start, and, with ending, begins.*

Life and time are a spiral, then, rather than merely a circle with its endless repetitions. T. S. Eliot, too, reminds us of this in "Little Gidding":

> *And the end of all our exploring*
> *Will be to arrive where we started*
> *And know the place for the first time.*[3]

When Maria and I parted, she was once again living in New Jersey near her children, where she had been when I first met her; and I returned to the same town of Larkspur, California. We are both back where we started, and yet not, for everything is different, starting with ourselves. In the eight years we were together, we inspired each other in our work of writing and speaking. Maria helped me feel more at home in the world of the humdrum every day, less identified with some idea of my own specialness, and yes, more open to the invisible workings of grace in a life. Love always changes us, whatever the eventual outcome of the relationship is. And overall, the love and the life I have shared with Maria have allowed me to feel more at home in my own skin, more at peace with the way things are and with who I am.

There were times soon after our parting when I thought I would never love again; when I felt that if this love, which had started so auspiciously, and had so much of the flavor of grace about it, could end, then nothing could be believed in anymore. There were moments when I felt cheated by life, fooled by my own fate. I was wrong, of course. Like Daphne, the nymph who transformed herself into a laurel tree to outwit the designs of Apollo, we too, against all odds, can miraculously enter another life. We have only to bow to the inevitable and become the wind. Eventually, and not always without a struggle, the wind is what I became.

2

GATE C22

by Ellen Bass

At gate C22 in the Portland airport
a man in a broad-band leather hat kissed
a woman arriving from Orange County.
They kissed and kissed and kissed. Long after
the other passengers clicked the handles of their carry-ons
and wheeled briskly toward short-term parking,
the couple stood there, arms wrapped around each other
like she'd just staggered off the boat at Ellis Island,
like she'd been released from ICU, snapped
out of a coma, survived bone cancer, made it down
from Annapurna in only the clothes she was wearing.

Neither of them was young. His beard was gray.
She carried a few extra pounds you could imagine
her saying she had to lose. But they kissed lavish
kisses like the ocean in the early morning,
the way it gathers and swells, sucking
each rock under, swallowing it
again and again. We were all watching—
passengers waiting for the delayed flight
to San Jose, the stewardesses, the pilots,

the aproned woman icing Cinnabons, the man selling
sunglasses. We couldn't look away. We could
taste the kisses crushed in our mouths.

But the best part was his face. When he drew back
and looked at her, his smile soft with wonder, almost
as though he were a mother still open from giving birth,
as your mother must have looked at you, no matter
what happened after—if she beat you or left you or
you're lonely now—you once lay there, the vernix
not yet wiped off, and someone gazed at you
as you were the first sunrise seen from the Earth.
The whole wing of the airport hushed,
all of us trying to slip into that woman's middle-
    aged body,
her plaid Bermuda shorts, sleeveless blouse, glasses,
little gold hoop earrings, tilting our heads up.

irresistible

This poem is irresistible, to my mind and ear, the way the words and the lines cascade down the page to end finally with an upturned face ready and open for a kiss to end all kisses. The rich, triumphant, and utterly unself-conscious images of sensual love at a certain age, in a public place, before the eyes of a gathering audience are an inspiration by example to throw away all cares about how others see us, to let our love and our passion be intrinsic to who we are, no less hidden than our appreciation for fine wine or delight at a sunset.

Ellen Bass is a fine and feisty West Coast poet who has been teaching creative writing in Santa Cruz for thirty years. Besides four volumes of poetry, she has written a number of nonfiction works, including *The Courage to Heal: A Guide for Women Survivors of Child Sexual Abuse,* which has sold more than a million copies worldwide, in ten languages. Her most recent poetry collection, *Mules of Love,* was the winner of the 2002 Lambda Literary Award for Poetry, and is full of the kind of passion and uninhibited exultation you can find in this poem, "Gate C22."

Love and sex are constant themes in her work, especially the kind that comes with age. In her poem "Jack Gottlieb's

in Love," she sings of an eighty-six-year-old man she knows
who's having more sex than the whole neighborhood:

> *Comes love.*
> *And all the cells in Jack's old organs stir.*
> *The heart, which had been ready to kick back*
> *and call it a day, signs on for another stint.*[1]

In "Sometimes, After Making Love," she speaks of

> *. . . breathing*
> *each other's breath, catching the wind*
> *in the sails of our bodies.*[2]

Bass's work is often deep, always poignant, frequently woven
with threads of grief and loss as well as starlight. And always,
always, so achingly human, which is why love is her subject
over and again.

The man in "Gate C22" is in Portland, Oregon, meeting
his love off a flight from Orange County. I know I'm making
assumptions that Bass may or may not have intended, but I
like to think that these two places are not thrown together
here by chance. Surely they mark the antipodes of liberal
and conservative thinking and lifestyles, as if to suggest that
love knows no boundaries, no politics, no race distinctions,
and certainly no age appropriateness. Love can fling the most
unlikely people into each other's arms, even if in the course
of time they increasingly find it a struggle to cope with their
emerging differences.

Love is also indifferent to its surroundings. This meeting takes place in an airport, perhaps one of the most soulless and arid places in modern life, which everyone is in a hurry to leave as soon as possible. But not these two. They savor their love right there in the arrival lounge, and seem ready to camp out there for the night. Their love spreads like a redemptive balm over the entire building. Everybody turns, forgetting their own preoccupations; they join in the joy.

> *They kissed and kissed and kissed.*

The repetition, but also the *K* sound (lips smacking), echoed in the next line with the clicking of carry-on handles, accentuates the couple's passion and marvelous lengthy absorption in their mutual delight. Were you ever as uninhibited as that? In an airport or a crowded elevator or a restaurant? I'm not sure that I have been. True, I will never forget my ex-wife greeting me in the airport dressed in a flimsy raincoat, which, I discovered when we got to short-term parking, and before we had climbed into the car, was the only item of clothing she had on; but as far as I am aware, there was no one else around in that moment but the two of us. And in fact I remember quite recently feeling self-conscious when a friend turned to embrace me, no holds barred, full lipped and luscious, in the middle of a crowded restaurant. I couldn't quite follow her there; not then, not in such a public place as my local eatery, even if it is Italian. *I'm* not Italian, after all (jokes about the English are not appropriate in this moment, and in any event are misinformed).

And how different this couple's pace and concerns are from those around them, who are walking briskly to short-term parking (though you never really know what goes on down there) with their smart black bags and business to attend to. There is nothing short term about these kissers; they have nowhere to go other than the spot they are in, and it seems they are in for the long haul. They are inhabiting a region of the brain wholly different from anywhere that might be described as brisk. They are each other's gift, and they are happy enough to take time with the wrapping, oblivious to the eyes of everyone around them.

I love the word *staggered* in this context. As if the woman from Orange County is a little tipsy, or is still feeling the effects of a roiling sea crossing. She's not in an ordinary state of consciousness. She is high on oxytocin, or serotonin, or probably both. She comes toward Portland man as if she had just woken from a coma, been given news that she will live after all, that the death sentence she thought her life was under had suddenly been lifted. All the images in this first stanza are ones of vibrant aliveness and wakening—you know the feeling. It's called love, when the veins are flooded with exotic substances from remote regions of the brain.

Now, it is common knowledge to those of a certain era that this sort of hormonal activity does not necessarily die down with the onset of age. Anna Swir, in her poem "The Greatest Love," describes being sixty and finding the greatest love of her life. She walks arm in arm with her beloved, hair stream-

ing in the wind, and he tells her that her hair is the color
of pearls.

> *Her children say:*
> *"Old fool."*[3]

But never mind being fifty, or sixty-something; remember
Jack Gottlieb, after all, revived suddenly at the age of eighty-
six. My friend's mother found love in her nursing home at
the age of eighty-four, and spiritual or brotherly love didn't
come into it. If you are thirty-something, you may wrinkle
your nose at the thought of it; but if your eighties are loom-
ing on the horizon, you will take cheer from such hearty
news. It's true that desire can slow down, and often disap-
pears altogether, but that is as likely to be the result of a long
marriage or developing estrangement as it is to physical in-
capacity. And love? Well, there's no reason, in Anna Swir's
poem or in this one by Bass, to suspect that love ever dies.

Nor does this kind of airport passion need beauty or ele-
gance to ignite it. This woman has a few extra pounds tucked
into her Bermuda shorts and sleeveless blouse, and her man
from Portland doesn't even notice. He's too busy kissing *lav-
ish kisses*. The wonderful image of rocks being sucked under
again and again by the rising tide gives us the feel, the sound,
the taste of their greedy embrace, tongues darting in and
out, pulling, sucking, letting go.

And all before an audience who could not look away. Why
could they not look away? Not, I think, because of some vi-
carious sexual thrill. That wasn't it. No, this couple's passion

and love were so unfettered, so innocent, so real that the only proper response was wonder and awe. As when a great storm suddenly breaks, all flashing and rumbling. As when you catch sight of the Grand Canyon for the very first time.

> *But the best part was his face. When he drew back*
> *and looked at her, his smile soft with wonder, almost*
> *as though he were a mother still open from giving birth.*

I don't know how you could conjure a better image for this moment than the one of a mother's face, fresh from giving birth: a fusion of orgasmic relaxation, sheer delight, wonder, relief, and marvel. He looks upon her as upon a new creation. As something, someone, made new, utterly new, whom he is seeing for the very first time.

And then the kiss, after all, is our first intimate touch, which begins with the feeding from our mother's breast. From that earliest beginning, nourishment, aggression, comfort, and sexuality are all intermingled in the intimate pleasures of the mouth. A kiss can be the door to another person's heart, and also the most intimate self-revelation. For this couple, it appears to be both.

Such a moment of supreme and tender openness is enough to cancel all the hurts and sorrows that may follow in a lifetime, Ellen Bass tells us in this poem. My own first glorious meeting with Maria changed me forever. It was worth everything that followed, and it exists as ever in my feeling for her today. I know this is how we hold each other, and always will. I am reminded of Jack Gilbert's poem in this book, "A Brief for the Defense," which ends with the lines

To hear the faint sound of oars in the silence as a rowboat
comes slowly out and then goes back is truly worth
all the years of sorrow that are to come.

There was almost certainly a time, whatever followed later, when your mother gazed at you

as you were the first sunrise seen from the Earth.

This is how the two people in the airport were seeing each other. In that moment, you know you are loved, accepted, and known completely. Everything else falls away. That kind of moment is one we all want to share. Every onlooker in that airport wants to climb into their middle-aged bodies.

The whole wing of the airport hushed, . . .

Hushed, because yes, there's something holy, sacred, about a moment like this, and everyone in the area is blessed in the presence of it. We become like baby birds, wanting as much as we can gather of this sweet nectar from the mother's breast, all of us,

tilting our heads up.

The mother is love itself, the great provider, sustainer, nourisher of body and soul. No wonder Ellen Bass had to sit down right there and then in the airport and write a poem, a soaring elegy, I would call it, to the delight and the relief of sharing these two people's joy, to the honor of being love's witness.

3

EACH MOMENT A WHITE BULL STEPS SHINING INTO THE WORLD

by Jane Hirshfield

If the gods bring to you
a strange and frightening creature,
accept the gift
as if it were one you had chosen.

Say the accustomed prayers,
oil the hooves well,
caress the small ears with praise.

Have the new halter of woven silver
embedded with jewels.
Spare no expense, pay what is asked,
when a gift arrives from the sea.

Treat it as you yourself
would be treated, brought speechless and naked
into the court of a king.

And when the request finally comes,
do not hesitate even an instant—

stroke the white throat,
the heavy, trembling dewlaps
you'd come to believe were yours,
and plunge in the knife.

Not once
did you enter the pasture
without pause,
without yourself trembling,
that you came to love it, that was the gift.

Let the envious gods take back what they can.

accept the gift

Even the title of this poem, all by itself, looms with signifi-
cance. We have heard many times, and in many different
ways, that life is a series of present moments rather than a
linear progression from past to future, that our one true life
can only really take place here where we are, and now. But
this title says far more than that, and with an image that,
once we have heard it, is liable to follow us everywhere, "like
a shadow or a friend," as Naomi Shihab Nye says in one of
her own poems, "Kindness."[1]

Each moment a white bull steps shining into the world.

Each moment is huge. Each moment comes bearing a
gift—or is it a curse?—from the gods, mighty and shining.
Someone somewhere will always be the recipient of it. One
moment the gift or the curse may be for you; the next mo-
ment, it may be for me. Shadowing this poem is the Greek
myth of Pasiphae, the Queen of King Minos of Crete.
Pasiphae fell under a spell cast by the sea god, Poseidon,
which resulted in her mating with a white bull. The progeny
of their union was the legendary Minotaur, the very monster

that Odysseus and also Theseus each had to confront many years later.

White bulls come in many forms. Often, we hope to pass them by. Even so, a bull—no ordinary bull, but a white one, pure, unsullied, fresh with the dew of heaven—is likely, at one time or another, to step forward, shining, into your life or mine. The bull is the epitome of strength, power, and libido. It offers us drive, direction, and purpose, a burst of new life.

It is also dangerous and frightening—frightening because you have probably never encountered such a wild beast before. Perhaps your life was coasting along—fulfilling enough, if fairly predictable. And then out of nowhere, in this very moment, something storms into your world that you cannot fail to notice; something strange, fascinating, overwhelming, even. And your comfortable, protecting circle is suddenly broken. Everything is thrown out of kilter, the center does not hold, the dishes are flying about the room.

This, precisely this, Jane Hirshfield suggests in her magnificent poem, is a gift from the gods. A gift, and not the curse we may take it to be. Our life asks us to accept it with as much grace as we are able—as if it were the very thing we would have chosen for ourselves. This kind of wildness storming into our living room could take the form of almost anything—a sudden illness, or loss of a loved one, perhaps; a spiritual awakening or crisis; a sudden reconfiguring of your work; and of course, the storm of love. Whatever breaks open the soul, pierces the lull of the daily round, is always a dangerous opportunity.

When it comes, as it will, Jane Hirshfield says in this poem, we should treat it as an honored guest, and welcome it with praises.

> *Spare no expense, pay what is asked,*
> *when a gift arrives from the sea.*

Pay what is asked. Such unexpected gifts come with a price, and we can only trust that it will be worth it—even if, when it first steps over our threshold, we would rather send it back. It is inconvenient right now; this is not the right time. It comes with too much prospect of pain and disruption. It would cause trouble to others. It spells the end of our life as we know it. The real price to pay, whatever our objections, will always be the surrender of our notion of control, which includes the surrender of our own opinions and objections to what we think is happening.

The gift, the second line quoted above tells us, *arrives from the sea.* The sea is the unconscious, the deep waters of our own life and being, where the light of our rational mind does not dare to venture. Poseidon, the god who gave Pasiphae her unexpected gift, ruled the sea. Anything that surges out of the unconscious will always be bigger than the ego's drive to shape experience the way it wants to see it. The price of new life, of a sudden influx of possibility from a direction never contemplated, is always surrender. And surrender means not only relinquishing resistance as we are hit by the wave, but also having no agenda for the way it will all turn out. Otherwise, we would be bargaining, and surrender is never a bargain you would want to make.

But we do bargain, of course; it's what the human ego does. Just one example of this is the best-selling *The Secret*, the publishing phenomenon that burst in on the zeitgeist a year or two ago. *The Secret* is only the latest in a very long line of products (*Think and Grow Rich*) that play in to our love of a bargain.[2] You think the right thoughts, and the world will deliver you the right response. You generate the field of attraction that corresponds to your desire, and you will attract the fruit of your desire. But a bargain is always and ever limited to the realm of the ego. The ego may indeed get what it wants, but then it will want something else, because its nature is to be ever hungry, never satisfied. So *The Secret* can never offer you more than what you already envision. It remains within the confines of your own strategic mind.

But the gift that erupts from the depths will be one you never bargained for. It will very likely seem more of a curse than anything else, especially to the one—the ego—who likes to be sure of what you are doing and where you are going. Had you known that this was what your life was going to give you, you might have run the other way a long time ago. Nevertheless, impossibly, it will come bearing a gift within the tribulation that may well shape your life from that moment on.

The white bull stormed into my own life in an unexpectedly gracious way several months after Maria and I parted. I was preparing to move to California when the Realtor brought over a woman interested in renting my New York apartment while I was away. She was in the apartment for three minutes. We did not speak or even look in each other's eyes. But the sight of her swung open a door in me that I never knew was there. As they left, I knew not only that she would take the apartment but that we would come to know each other in a way that would change us. (No, this is not leading to another fairy-tale ending.)

But why did I know that, or rather know and feel that? There was no external evidence of any kind. How difficult these things are to shape into words. She was beautiful, yes— tall, lithe, graceful, her dark hair framing softly chiseled features, a full, generous mouth, and unusually large eyes. I acknowledge being an easy prey for beauty, and especially of her kind, the anima figure incarnate; but I was living in the West Village; beautiful women walked past my door every day without my feeling they were about to walk into my life in some way. Quite simply, I do not think I have ever felt what I was feeling there in my apartment that day—or indeed what I have continued to feel since.

All I can say is that there was something about the way her eyes followed an upward gaze, as a faint smile turned the corners of her mouth. I was particularly struck by the way she took in my two armchairs, which are covered in an old-fashioned pattern of large roses. It was as if they were familiar to her somehow; in fact, the whole apartment (such as it is, some 350 square feet of Manhattan turf) seemed to be known to her already. I felt as if she knew me, knew my sensibility, my way of being in the world. I felt seen, known. Which of course was ridiculous. She hadn't even looked at me. But there it is; that is what I felt as she walked back out of the door, leaving me to sit down in my rose armchair feeling suddenly very quiet, and somewhat disoriented; feeling that it wasn't just a tenant who was walking downstairs.

I had also been disoriented when I first met Maria. I was astonished at her open gaze and strong, tender presence. But far from feeling some recognition for her, I couldn't fathom who she was. She was like a magnificent apparition from some other world than the one I had lived in until that time. She was both wonderful and foreign. When meeting Patricia, the woman who walked in my door that day, I felt lifted into an immediate and intimate familiarity, without any word spoken or glance exchanged. It was not an emotional experience so much as a feeling of unusual quiet descending on me.

We next met when I returned to New York to pack my personal things for California. We agreed to exchange keys and the lease over dinner. That dinner lasted five hours. At one moment, I heard myself saying that I would do anything for her. I stopped in astonishment at what I had just said, and what I knew it meant for me. It meant that, in that moment at least, I would go anywhere, do anything, drop life as I knew it to follow her if that was what she wanted of me. If she were to ask me to catch the next flight to France with her, I would settle the check and leave immediately (in the event, it was *she* who insisted on paying for dinner that night); if she wanted me to pour myself into the nonprofit she had just started, I would do that; if it were to get up and leave the restaurant in that moment and never see her again, I would do that as well. I told her it was madness to say such a thing, to seem to give myself over to a woman I had known all of a few hours, and who (damn!), I had discovered in the course of our conversation, was married. But it was too late. Those were the words that spilled from my mouth. And they seemed not to shock her at all, as if she knew from her own experience what I meant, but that she also knew that contingent reality would have it otherwise.

In the year following that dinner, I have come to learn how to love someone without holding them; to acknowledge (both to her and to myself) the deepest *Yes!* I had ever felt for anyone, and yet to accept at the same time that our love was of the soul and spirit, not to be actualized in everyday reality. And, yes, you may be right, her unavailability may be the reason I could say that *yes* so readily. Personally, however, and as you may imagine, I do not warm to that conclusion. What stormed into my living room doesn't feel conditional in that way. The *yes* was, and remains, to who she is in her totality, including the contingencies of her everyday life.

She did not stray for a second from her commitment to her marriage, and I did not for a moment attempt to seduce her either into physical intimacy or away from her husband— not because I am an unusually evolved example of the species *Homo erectus,* but because it was so clear from the start that this was the only possible way we could continue to have any relationship at all. She said as much during that first dinner. She knew as well as I did that "a strange and frightening creature" had come into our lives, a gift from the gods that could not be denied, and we needed to find some way to honor it. Over the following year we would meet whenever I came to New York, most days I was there, for coffee, for lunch, for a stroll along Bleecker Street, for the occasional movie. She told her husband whenever we met, and when I eventually met him myself, I thanked him for his latitude in supporting our deepening friendship. "She loves you," he said. "And I trust her."

His trust is not misplaced, even though in California, there was barely a moment when Patricia was not in my awareness. There have been times when I have been angry with myself for even giving her a moment's thought. I knew full well the implications of falling in love with someone who is unavailable—that it is likely to be self-destructive, self-defeating, and ultimately profoundly unsatisfying. But mostly, this was far from unsatisfying, despite the poignancy of the situation and the inevitable pain. On the contrary, in saying yes to the reality of my feelings for this woman, I have allowed myself to be as undefended as I have ever known with another human being, even more so since no tangible outcome—no payback—is feasible. So I was able to experience what it is like to love without expecting anything in return. I have been able, and I don't know why, or how, to honor the gift and to pay what was asked, the bittersweet pain of loving someone I could never be with.

Of course I fantasized; of course I imagined, especially to begin with, our lives changing in such a way that would eventually make it possible for us to come together. And of course I liked to think that she did, too. But even from the beginning, and increasingly over time, I knew this was a different kind of love. I knew I was not going to *get* something from it, in terms of fulfilled desire. It became a fire that is, still now,

burning up the longing itself, my fantasies of some rosy out-
come, and is leaving me, not hopeless—far from it—but alive
in a way that can embrace the beloved without having or
holding her; that can feel, intuit, the beloved as an inner
experience, independent of anyone else. As Rumi says,

> *Your pure longing,*
> *That is the secret cup.*
> *The grief you cry out from*
> *draws you toward union.*[3]

As I write, my love now for Patricia is something ever pres-
ent; she is not separate from myself, and so I am not haunted
by a sense of absence (even though, paradoxically, I can't
wait to see her whenever I can); nor am I longing for some
future outcome that is different from what is so now. This
has brought with it a profound relief, a restfulness in which
I can only feel blessed to know her. It is the rest that comes
with fully acknowledging the way things are, instead of main-
taining a struggle to have them be different. It has, however,
taken many painful weeks and months to arrive at this. And
even now, I don't take it for granted. These feelings are bigger
than I am, and I am learning to treat them with the respect
and honor that such a gift from the gods deserves. Ultimately,
I can only bow to the fact that I am not in control when it
comes to white bulls appearing from nowhere.

I do know, though, that within its given limits, I have given
this love my all without trying to corral it, or rationalize it,
and without trying to take it somewhere it cannot go. After

all, the only thing I have risked losing is face—looking like
a fool—and I never really needed that anyway. It is as if I
myself had been

> . . . brought speechless and naked
> into the court of a king.

Though in my case the royal personage was a queen. And
yes, it is true that for a while I also risked losing the opportu-
nity to meet someone who was available, because my heart
was already taken, with someone I was barely able to touch.
Gradually, though, my feelings for Patricia have become ab-
sorbed into my being. They are a part of who I am now,
rather than something that is taking up space.

What I have just described is the gradual acceptance that
the form of this gift, if not its essence, has eventually and in-
evitably to be offered up to something greater than my own
needs and desires. The gods will take back what was in reality
always theirs. After all, everything in this world is only on
loan to us, but especially something like this, where the loan
is evident from the start in the rules of encounter.

> And when the request finally comes, . . .

There was not one moment but many moments during
which I came gradually to acknowledge the truth of what I
had fallen into. The request inherent from the start was that
I acknowledge the impossibility of this love ever having a con-
crete form while at the same time not diminishing the truth
of its existence, that I accept that it would need to find an ex-
pression that honored our different realities as we lived them.

That was the knife that was required to cut through any false hopes I might have had—and I certainly had them. Perhaps this sounds all too close to an exercise in self-punishment, and at times I have wondered precisely that, especially in the moments—and they have come—of dramatizing obsession.

But self-punishment happens only within the small circle of the ego. This is a love that is both personal and beyond the personal. The whole joy of it is that it is bigger than I am, that I cannot separate it into either a spiritual or a personal love. It is both at the same time. Any great love is like this, which is why it has wings to lift us beyond our self-preoccupations; which, if we pay attention and treat it that way, is why it is one of the greatest spiritual gifts.

All this describes why we never go into the pasture where the white bull lives

> *without pause,*
> *without yourself trembling, . . .*

We tremble because we are in the presence of the numinous, whether its face be the face of death, of great loss, or of a great love. We can have no idea of the eventual outcome of such an encounter. All we can know is that we will not come out of that pasture as the person who went in. We will not be who we once were, and our life will not be what it once was. The only true response to the numinous is awe, and even dread, as when Moses beheld the Burning Bush. And then this decisive line:

> *that you came to love it, that was the gift.*

Yes, yes! That is the gift! That is why we can let the gods take back whatever remains—the form of the gift—because the essence of it can never be taken away from us, the love that has burst open our heart and ushered in a deeper, more vital way of living. And this is why the gods are *envious:* For all the everlasting pleasures of immortality they enjoy, they will never know the poignant yet ephemeral delights of the flesh. They will never know the tangible love that we can know for another human being, for a place, for a dog or a river. Nor will they ever know the heartbreaking sadness that will come with its loss.

They can only look on as we suffer the knowledge that everything that is given is also taken away. They can only envy our little cries of longing—essays like this one, and our poems, our music, our great epics and songs—as we are cooked in the fire of love, stewed in our own juices, so to speak; they can only wonder what it must be like to be so achingly human as, God willing (nothing is certain), we emerge more tender and open into the light of a new day.

The Heart's True Home

We had a West Highland Terrier for a number of years. "Westies" are tough little dogs, bred to tunnel into badger holes and engage the "enemy" in its lair. Our Westie was many generations removed from her origins, but she still retained that instinct, put into her through years of breeding. On one occasion she became obsessed by some "critter" under a rock in our backyard. Nothing could dissuade her. She dug and dug until she tunneled several feet under the rock.

> TODAY'S READING
> **Ecclesiastes 3:10–11**
>
> **[God] has . . . set eternity in the human heart.**
> Ecclesiastes 3:11

Now consider this question: Why do we as humans pursue, pursue, pursue? Why must we climb unclimbed mountains, ski near-vertical slopes? Run the most difficult and dangerous rapids, challenge the forces of nature? Part of it is a desire for adventure and enjoyment, but it's much more. It's an instinct for God that has been implanted in us. We cannot *not* want to find God.

We don't know that, of course. We only know that we long for something. "You don't know what it is you want," Mark Twain said, "but you want it so much you could almost die."

God is our heart's true home. As church father Augustine said in that most famous quotation: "You have made us for Yourself, O Lord, and our hearts are restless until they rest in You."

And what is the heart? A deep void within us that only God can fill. 🌿

DAVID ROPER

Help me, Lord, to recognize my deep longing for You. Then fill me with the knowledge of You. Draw me near.

Beneath all our longings is a deep desire for God.

Harvest and Thanksgiving

Several thousand years ago, God spoke directly to Moses and instituted a new festival for His people. In Exodus 23:16, according to Moses's record, God said, "Celebrate the Festival of Harvest with the firstfruits of the crops you sow in your field."

Today countries around the world do something similar by celebrating the land's bounty. In Ghana, the people celebrate the Yam Festival as a harvest event. In Brazil, *Dia de Acao de Gracas* is a time to be grateful for the crops that yielded their food. In China, there is the Mid-Autumn (Moon) Festival. In the United States and Canada: Thanksgiving.

> **TODAY'S READING**
> **Genesis 8:15–9:3**
>
> **Celebrate the Festival of Harvest with the firstfruits of the crops you sow in your field.**
> Exodus 23:16

To understand the fitting goal of a harvest celebration, we visit Noah right after the flood. God reminded Noah and his family—and us—of His provision for our flourishing existence on the earth. Earth would have seasons, daylight and darkness and "seedtime and harvest" (GEN. 8:22). Our gratitude for the harvest, which sustains us, goes to God alone.

No matter where you live or how you celebrate your land's bounty, take time today to express gratitude to God—for we would have no harvest to celebrate without His grand creative design. 🌳

DAVE BRANON

Dear Creator God, thank You so much for the wondrous way You fashioned this world—with seasons, with harvest-time, with everything we need to exist. Please accept our gratitude.

f What are you thankful for?
Share at **Facebook.com/ourdailybread**.

Gratitude is the memory of a glad heart.

4

LEAVING MT. BALDY

by Leonard Cohen

I come down from the mountain
after many years of study
and rigorous practice.
I left my robes hanging on a peg
in the old cabin
where I had sat so long
and slept so little.
I finally understood
I had no gift
for Spiritual Matters.
"Thank you Beloved,"
I heard a heart cry out
as I entered the stream of cars
on the Santa Monica Freeway,
westbound for L.A.
A number of people
(some of them practitioners)
have begun to ask me angry questions
about the Ultimate Reality.
I suppose they don't like to see
old Jikan smoking.

down from the mountain

This may not be an obvious "change your life" poem, but like nearly all of Leonard Cohen's poetry, it is permeated with both the humility that comes with true spiritual insight and also the realization that this world we live in is not different, and not better or worse, than the world conjured by our spiritual aspirations. For those engaged in some kind of spiritual practice, this poem can be an awakening bell to remind us that there is no world other than the one we are in now, that our attempts to escape it or transcend it are likely to come from some more or less subtle arrogance on our part that prompts us to look down on people and actions that do not fit our "spiritual" view of how life should be.

Leonard Cohen is best known as a singer/songwriter, but he was a poet long before he hit the mainstream in the 1960s with his grave, tuneless, and, for many, irresistible low drone of a voice that sang of lost loves and loneliness. It was probably more for the tone of his voice than the actual content of his songs, which are in fact more often than not songs of praise to life in this world, that he became known as "the godfather of gloom." He was born in 1934 in Montreal, and published his first collection of poetry, *Let Us Compare Mythologies,* in 1956. He soon moved to the Greek island of Hydra, where he remained for several years and wrote two highly successful novels and more poetry. Then in the mid-sixties he started to write songs. He came to America and met Judy Collins, who launched his spectacular singer/ songwriter career by including his song "Suzanne" on one of her albums.

Besides his evident love of women and beauty, one of the themes that has pervaded all of his work from the very beginning is what he calls, in his novel *Beautiful Losers,* the theme of Tibetan Desire, "the unholy union between renunciation and longing and the difficulty in divorcing one from the other."[1] Cohen's mentor in poetry was Irving Layton, the great Canadian poet who died in 2006, and Cohen's most recent poetry collection, *The Book of Longing* (published in 2006), is dedicated to him. Layton once said that "a poet is deeply conflicted and it is in his work that he reconciles those deep conflicts. It doesn't set the world in order, it doesn't really change anything. It just is a kind of harbor, it's the place of reconciliation, the kiss of peace."[2] This is what I feel Cohen's poems to be, safe harbors for those who hear in their own lives the echoes of his loves and struggles. Tibetan Desire shows up in practically every one of the poems in *The Book of Longing,* which includes "Leaving Mt. Baldy." Most of the poems reflect his experience as a monk during the five years or so he spent near Los Angeles at Mt. Baldy Zen Center, the monastery he left in 1999.

I came down from the mountain

is a literal statement, then, but it is also a metaphor, something of a self-parody. Cohen is coming down from his high notions of what *spirituality* means, coming back to join ordinary life and people on earth. He practiced hard and long, as is the Zen way. He gave it his all. But after several years of putting on twenty pounds of robes every morning at 2:30 A.M.

over my enormous hard-on

(as he says in the poem "Early Morning at Mt. Baldy"), he realizes it is time to call it a day and hang up those robes on their peg and leave them there for the next spiritual warrior.[3]

But the literal meaning of the line is equally significant. For all his self-deprecation, Cohen is not merely another guy stuck in a traffic jam westbound for L.A. He has just put in five years or more of hard spiritual practice on that mountain. He has more than a notion of the way his mind works. He is able to rejoin the messiness of ordinary life and appreciate its beauty precisely because he has done the work of seeing the way his mind constructs reality, with all its notions of good and bad and right and wrong. He's reenacting the old Zen ox-herding story, in which the herder, on starting his journey, sees mountains; then, as he moves along the way, he sees that there are no mountains or anything else outside of his own perception; finally, as he returns home, he sees the mountains again after all.

Cohen leaves the robes behind, and in doing so leaves behind any sense of schism between one world and the next. He will not bring a badge with him to wear as a spiritual identity in the messy, confusing world the rest of us live in.

> *I finally understood*
> *I had no gift*
> *For Spiritual Matters.*

Why has he capitalized these last two words? As he has also done later on with the phrase *Ultimate Reality*? He seems to be casting an ironic glance at the very notions these terms intend to convey, looking askance at the idea that there are some matters that are spiritual and some that are not, that there is some Reality that is ultimate and another that is not. In the Zen view, after all, This is *It*! This—who and where we are now—is it! There is no greater secret waiting to be revealed than this.

So Leonard Cohen assures us he has no gift for Spiritual Matters. Except that this very statement suggests otherwise. It was T. S. Eliot who said once that the only lesson we can hope to learn is humility. "Humility," Eliot said, "is endless." Far from being a failure, Cohen seems to have grasped the root of the matter.

To my mind these lines also suggest that spiritual matters ultimately transcend any comparison with a profession. You can become a priest, all right, or even a monk, as Cohen did, and consider it your chosen way. But in the end, nothing works; no strategy, bargaining, or crafty moves will get you there. The robes won't get you there, wherever "there" is.

Which doesn't mean you don't bother to do anything. Practice does make a difference; Cohen's time on the mountain changed him. But at the same time, there is no surefire technique to enlightenment, or salvation, because all techniques remain by their nature within the province of the mind and the personal will. True, the prayer or the practice may serve to launch you into a condition where the personal will is left behind, where what the Tibetans call *Rigpa* and the Japanese call *satori,* or insight, or what the Christians call grace, allows you to see the fundamental unity of all life, beyond any division of subject and object; and that life unfolds perfectly naturally on its own without the exercise of your will.

In Soto Zen, they speak of enlightenment in a way that conjures a phrase of Yeats—"the peace that comes dropping slow"—like fine rain, which is not so very different in orientation from mystical Christians' "waiting on God." It's not in our hands, in other words. We can prepare the ground, but spiritual insight is not an achievement so much as a grace that we cannot take any credit for. This is one of the realizations Cohen is taking with him down the mountain. In another poem, "Pardon Me," he says,

> *Pardon me if I receive the Holy Spirit*
> *without telling you about it.*[4]

And in "Anything Which Refers," he says, in true Zen style,

> *Anything which refers to the matter, even*
> *obliquely, is far from the mark.*[5]

You might wonder why a Buddhist would hear a heart that cries out,

Thank you Beloved.

Well, Leonard Cohen did not become a Buddhist. He is Jewish, and always said the old religion suited him fine. His poems are full of the *G-d* word, and if ever there was anyone who identified with the lover-beloved story, it was him. He was in a Zen monastery because he liked how he felt when in the company of the abbot Joshu Sasaki Roshi:

> *When I eat meat with Roshi*
> *the four-legged animals*
> *don't cry any more*
> *and the two-legged animals*
> *don't try to fly away.*[6]

In "Early Questions," he says,

> *Why do you command us to talk, and then talk instead?*
> *It is because a bell has summoned me to your room, it is*
> *because I am speechless in the honour of your company, it*
> *is because I am reeling in the fragrance of some unutterable*
> *hospitality, it is because I have forgotten all my questions,*
> *that I throw myself to the floor, and vanish into yours.*[7]

What a lover this man is! It is Cohen's own heart that cries out in gratitude as he finally leaves the mountain and descends

into the morning traffic bound for L.A. The traffic is the per-
fect metaphor for everyday life's humbling and humdrum
ordinariness; and yet an appreciation for that, and for his
own ordinariness, is precisely what he came to experience up
there gazing at the white wall all day long. Nothing is more
real than everyday experience, which constantly invites us to
let go of any spiritual persona we may have carefully devel-
oped and cherished over the years and to join everyone else
in the chaos and the light and the dark of this imperfect
world.

There is something else, though, that may be more than a
coincidence: It is the freeway that Cohen joins on leaving the
monastery. The whole point of the monastic life is freedom:
freedom from duality, freedom from the convictions of one's
own mind. And in joining the world again, Cohen finds him-
self on the freeway.

His time with Roshi did not dissolve the chaos in his own
mind; nor did he ever suppose that Roshi himself was always
impeccable and ever free from all inconsistency. In the novel
Beautiful Losers, written some thirty years before his time on
Mt. Baldy, he suggests that

> contact with this energy (love) results in the exer-
> cise of a kind of balance in the chaos of existence.
> A saint does not dissolve chaos; if he did the world
> would have changed long ago. I do not think that a
> saint dissolves the chaos even for himself, for there
> is something arrogant in the notion of a man set-
> ting the universe in order. It is a kind of balance

that is his glory. He rides the drifts like an escaped
ski. . . . Something in him so loves the world that he
gives himself to the laws of gravity and chance. Far
from flying with angels, he traces with the fidelity
of a seismograph needle the state of the solid
blood landscape. He can love the shape of human
beings, the fine and twisted shapes of the heart. It
is good to have among us such men, such balanc-
ing monsters of the heart.

How prescient this passage is of his time with Joshu Sasaki
Roshi, and his descent from the mountain. Instead of imply-
ing even in the smallest way that he may have developed
some spiritual insight, Cohen expresses in many different
ways the kind of sentiment to be found in the poem "Titles,"
where he tells us that though he looked the part of the
monk, with the shaved head and the heavy robes,

> *I hated everyone*
> *But I acted generously*
> *And no one found me out.*[8]

Perhaps he left the monastery because he felt it was time
in his life for a woman again, and for his beloved cigarettes.
Throughout his life, he has taken the advice of his friend
Sheila seriously (these two lines are from his poem "What Do
You Really Remember"):

> *She said, "Don't be a jerk, Len.*
> *Take your desire seriously."*[9]

Cohen has written several poems about cigarettes, including one called "The Cigarette Issue," so the subject has probably been one he's felt ambivalence about for a long time. It appears he is not the only one. Having spent a few years in a monastery, he should be something of an authority on matters spiritual, right? So, naturally, others will start asking him questions of a spiritual nature, perhaps even more understandably since he happens to be Leonard Cohen. But they ask angrily, the poem says. They are conflicted. And probably because they cannot reconcile a spiritual authority with someone who smokes. And old Jikan, as Cohen calls himself here (Jikan, meaning Silent One, was the name he was given at the monastery) smokes, and quite frequently. That would be a problem for someone who has definite ideas about what it means to be spiritual. It is a problem he confronts in his short poem "What Did It," in which he speaks of the Indian sage Nisargadatta Maharaj offering a cigarette to a Western student. The student declined, saying he didn't smoke.

"Don't smoke?" said the master.
"What's life for?"[10]

Which of course is not so much a defense of smoking as it is a challenge to fixed beliefs about what is spiritual and what isn't. I have never smoked myself. The world I have lived in has generally been smoke free. I know it smacks of a rarefied existence, which is not in fact true on other counts, but I own up to this particular rarefaction. So it would be normal then, wouldn't it, for me to have developed *opinions* about

smoking and smokers—opinions that are self-evidently cor-
rect, of course, which must make me ever so slightly superior
to those who indulge the dirty habit.

I had no need to become aware of my own opinions until
my ex-wife decided to take up smoking for the first time a
few years into our marriage. I had always considered her to
be unusually endowed with a natural wisdom, until the
smoke started to curl around her nostrils. Then I started to
wonder. Then I started to think she was losing it. I mean,
who in their right mind . . . ? She, however, was impressively
unperturbed by my opinions, and indeed by the opinions of
pretty much everyone else she knew. So my opinions began
to bounce back to me. Then I began to realize that they were
more of an accurate commentary on my own state of mind
than on hers. After a few months, it ceased mattering to me
whether she smoked or not, which, again, was more of a relief
to me than it was to her. Quite simply, it was not my business.
Besides, it was yet another humbling lesson on the abiding
truth that we can never change anyone other than ourselves,
and that to attempt to do so is merely to invite nothing but
suffering and disappointment for all involved.

My misconception was that there are some things that are
innately against the love of an examined life. This is the mis-
conception that Cohen's angry questioners had. Underlying
our false notion is an implicit schism between body and
spirit. The only true renunciation, however, is not of this or
that habit, but of the experience and idea of separation itself.
This is the wisdom in this poem, in which Leonard Cohen
values his place in the traffic jam—on the freeway—as much

as his monastery cabin. When we no longer distance our-
selves from anything or anyone, when we give equal value to
this messy world and the world of spirit, we may catch the
scent of what Rumi refers to when he says

> Out beyond ideas
> Of wrongdoing and rightdoing
> There is a field. I'll meet you there.[11]

5

WHAT THE LIVING DO
by Marie Howe

Johnny, the kitchen sink has been clogged for days,
   some utensil probably fell down there.
And the Drano won't work but smells dangerous, and
   the crusty dishes have piled up

waiting for the plumber I still haven't called. This is
   the everyday we spoke of.
It's winter again: the sky's a deep headstrong blue, and
   the sunlight pours through

the open living room windows because the heat's on too
   high in here, and I can't turn it off.
For weeks now, driving, or dropping a bag of groceries
   in the street, the bag breaking,

I've been thinking: This is what the living do. And
   yesterday, hurrying along those
wobbly bricks in the Cambridge sidewalk, spilling my
   coffee down my wrist and sleeve,

I thought it again, and again later, when buying a
  hairbrush: This is it.
Parking. Slamming the car door shut in the cold. What
  you called that yearning.

What you finally gave up. We want the spring to come
  and the winter to pass. We want
whoever to call or not call, a letter, a kiss—we want
  more and more and then more of it.

But there are moments, walking, when I catch a
  glimpse of myself in the window glass,
say, the window of the corner video store, and I'm
  gripped by a cherishing so deep

for my own blowing hair, chapped face, and unbuttoned
  coat that I'm speechless:

I am living, I remember you.

the cherishing

Marie Howe's poetry is a luminous exploration of love and loss, the one shot through, like silk, with the other. And gratitude, awakening, living again; it is all here in this poem, the title poem of her collection published in 1998. Johnny is her brother, who died of AIDS some time before the collection was published, and much of the book is dedicated to him.

After his death (and perhaps even before), Johnny became an intimate guide through life for Howe, and many of her poems are testimony to the things he showed her. In "The Last Time," she has him say,

> *I'm going to die soon. I want you to know that.*

She's puzzled, because she already knows that, and says so.

> *And he said, No, I mean that you are.*[1]

Then the poem "The Gate" begins with the lines

> *I had no idea that the gate I would step through*
> *To finally enter this world*
> *Would be the space my brother's body made . . .*[2]

As if in some mysterious way his passing brought her finally and solidly into the world of the living. For many of us, perhaps, it may not be surprising that Marie Howe should have spent her life up until that time not so fully convinced that this world was where she wanted to be. After all, it's not so easy here, and our loftier thoughts can easily aspire to some kinder realm of light where we feel we really belong. The body creaks and groans and can have trouble digesting dinner; it anchors us in a world of limits. Whereas the ideal world of the spirit, or the mind—not quite of this world but not out of the body either—seems to beckon with endless possibilities, and the promise of beauty, goodness, truth, there for the asking. At the heart of this poem, "What the Living Do," and in a brilliant flash of poetic imagination, Howe succeeds in bringing these two worlds together in their true creative relationship.

Don't you just know that feeling, when the sink has been clogged for over a week and you just haven't seemed to find the time to call the plumber? Or when the heating is turned up high for winter but you have to open the windows because you can't manage to turn the heat off or down? Life always seems to have something going on that shouldn't be going on—not, at least, in the life we imagined for ourselves. There is always some hitch in our best-laid plans. This is the everyday. This is the way it is, and we rather wish it were otherwise. Wouldn't life be so much better if things just *worked*, if we could get from here to there without something unexpected or uncalled-for sticking its head in the way?

But no, stuff happens; we drop our bag of groceries and the bag breaks. We hurry down

those wobbly bricks in the Cambridge sidewalk, . . .

and our coffee spills down our wrist and stains our sleeve, the sleeve that perhaps we had laundered only yesterday. But, Marie Howe says in this poem, *This is what the living do.* It's normal for things to fall apart, to be dropped, to not quite work, to take a left instead of the right turn we intended. *This is what the living do;* it's intrinsic to life itself, and not only that, we will see that the fault line is precisely the clue, the secret, to the fulfillment we are always seeking.

Our blessing and also our curse is that we are born into two worlds, not quite belonging to either. We have animal bodies and instincts, we are subject to the law and limitations of gravity; and at the same time, we have a mind that can envision infinite possibilities, that wants us to fly like angels. Rilke says this wonderfully in his poem "Sunset":

> *. . . sometimes blocked in, sometimes reaching out,*
> *one moment your life is a stone in you, and the*
> *next, a star.*[3]

The tension between these two realities that live in us sets up a longing for a condition, a life, without struggle, for our own image of paradise. *That yearning,* as Howe's brother Johnny called it, comes with the package of being human;

it's in our hard drive. Something always seems to be missing,
even if we can't put our finger on it. And because it's not easy
to identify, we can easily blame it on conditions. Life will be
so much better when the spring comes and this terrible win-
ter is finally over. It will be better when someone calls,
when . . . when . . . the list goes on and on, it's endless. When
I am in New York, I wonder about Paris. When I am in Paris,
I think of London. Show me a map of the Mediterranean,
and all my longings will flutter up like sand swallows.

Marie Howe's spilling her coffee, not calling the plumber,
slamming shut the car door in winter, all this grates and rubs
and causes the yearning for something different, for a world
where the living is easy. Because, as Zen teacher and psycho-
therapist John Tarrant says in his book *The Light Inside the
Dark* (1999), "spirit forgets the necessity of imperfection,
and that within our very incompleteness is the opening where
love appears. It does not understand the essentially domestic
and mortal nature of human life."

And yet, this is exactly what Howe does come to under-
stand in this poem. In sharing with us the little imperfec-
tions and foibles of her daily life, she somehow celebrates
those very things she is apparently protesting against. The
imperfections of her day are the very things that make her
human, that draw us close to her, and allow us, the reader, to
feel empathy, and even love, for her and our human condi-
tion in general. We can empathize with her because we all
have a fault line, and usually one with many branches. It will
always be that way, and always has. Even mighty Achilles had
his heel. And doesn't Venus de Milo look better without her

arms? Imagine her up there at the top of that staircase in the Louvre, complete and intact. No, it just wouldn't work.

The poet Ellery Akers speaks to the longing (for the perfect, the finished) in us in a poem called "Advice from an Angel":

> *I know it's in your nature to want air,*
> *ozone. To float; to be free. But stick with what you know:*
> *you'd be surprised at the effect of sheer blundering*
> *and doggedness. To evaporate is nothing:*
> *to sprint, to travel. It's weight*
> *that divides the known and unknown worlds. It's your boots*
> *that impress us, your squads of boulders . . .*[4]

In his ninth elegy of the *Duino Elegies*, Rilke says,

> *Praise the world*
> *to the angel,*
> *not the unsayable.*[5]

And this, I believe, is exactly what Howe is doing in this poem. She runs through a litany of mistakes and failings, only to endear both them and herself to us. She leads on naturally to our common response to such obstructions, which is our longing, our wish, for some better state. But that longing is exactly what her brother, now without a body, has given up. And then she, too, toward the close of the poem, delights in giving it up. There are moments, she says, when she catches sight of herself in a window (not an elegant window, a Barneys or a Marc Jacobs window, but the window of the corner video store, oh so drab and humdrum):

. . . and I'm gripped by a cherishing so deep

for my own blowing hair, chapped face, and
unbuttoned coat that I'm speechless:

I am living, I remember you.

She marvels at the fact of her own living, her own beauti-
ful, imperfect form walking past. And in that speechless mo-
ment, she redeems this broken world, she redeems her own
imperfect life, she does what Rilke urges us to do: to praise
this world, to sing its praises out loud so even the angels can't
fail to hear us. And in her praising, Marie Howe stitches the
two worlds that live in us all back together again.

To praise the imperfect, the ordinary, is not something
that comes easily to us in the Western world, wedded as
we are to the idea of the new, the young, the latest innova-
tion. But in Japan there is an entire worldview that appre-
ciates the value of the imperfect, unfinished, and faulty.
It's called wabi-sabi, where the first term refers to some-
thing simple and unpretentious, and the second points to
the beauty that comes with age. Wabi-sabi is the aesthetic
view that underlies traditional Japanese art forms like the tea
ceremony, calligraphy, and ceramics. It's an aesthetic that
sees beauty in the modest and humble, the irregular and
earthy. It holds that beauty comes with the patina of age and
in the changes that come with use. It lies in the cracks, the
worn spots, in the green corrosion of bronze, the pattern of
moss on a stone. The Japanese take pleasure in mistakes and
imperfections.

In that moment of catching her reflection in a window, Howe realizes with a start that she is living, and in that very same moment, she remembers her brother, who is dead. He reminds her that she is not built to last. Day by day, tiny specks of us float away. No matter which exercise regimen we follow, no matter which self-help guru we believe in, nothing will dispel the reality that death is our supreme limitation, the final proof that perfection was never meant to be part of the human experience. A hundred years from now, all new people. Sooner, rather than later, we shall not be here: no eyes, no blowing hair, no chapped face, no unbuttoned coat, no you or me—gone, who knows where, if anywhere.

Yet it is just this knowledge of her soon-not-to-be-here-ness, felt in that moment of seeing, that wakes up Howe to the miracle that she is here at all. In that moment of seeing, Marie Howe cherishes—such a tender, beautiful word—the life that has been given her. She holds it in her heart and her hands and blesses it for the precious gift that it is. And if the clogged sink and spilled coffee and hairbrush buying are part of it, all well and good; it's all worth it, everything is worth it just to be here, here where angels can never tread, never taste, touch, feel, smell the coffee as we do. And if you think about it, that is the brilliance of the human design plan: The built-in "defect" of mortality is the very thing that can spur us to drink down the full draft as it comes to us, whatever shape or form it comes in.

How did this happen? This incredible feeling/thinking/sensing/moving/joyous/painful/doubting/wondering life—what keeps it upright even now, right now in this unrepeatable moment that is already going, gone? No answer to that, merely the gasp of the breath as it moves in and out, and the pleasure of knowing that we are here and not elsewhere. Better to taste it now, then, this life that we have, than to defer it to some future that may never come—however imperfect it may seem to us in passing. For as Leonard Cohen says in one of his songs,

> *There is a crack, a crack in everything.*
> *That's how the light gets in.*[6]

6

A BRIEF FOR THE DEFENSE
by Jack Gilbert

Sorrow everywhere. Slaughter everywhere. If babies
are not starving someplace, they are starving
somewhere else. With flies in their nostrils.
But we enjoy our lives because that's what God wants.
Otherwise the mornings before summer dawn would not
be made so fine. The Bengal tiger would not
be fashioned so miraculously well. The poor women
at the fountain are laughing together between
the suffering they have known and the awfulness
in their future, smiling and laughing while somebody
in the village is very sick. There is laughter
every day in the terrible streets of Calcutta,
and the women laugh in the cages of Bombay.
If we deny our happiness, resist our satisfaction,
we lessen the importance of their deprivation.
We must risk delight. We can do without pleasure,
but not delight. Not enjoyment. We must have
the stubbornness to accept our gladness in the ruthless
furnace of this world. To make injustice the only
measure of our attention is to praise the Devil.

If the locomotive of the Lord runs us down,
we should give thanks that the end had magnitude.
We must admit there will be music despite everything.
We stand at the prow again of a small ship
anchored late at night in the tiny port
looking over to the sleeping island: the waterfront
is three shuttered cafés and one naked light burning.
To hear the faint sound of oars in the silence as a rowboat
comes slowly out and then goes back is truly worth
all the years of sorrow that are to come.

we must risk delight

"A Brief for the Defense"? Funny title, you might think, for a poem on joy. But Jack Gilbert is right: Joy needs defending. It can indeed seem up for trial without a defense in times like ours, when the world's miseries and injustices are clamoring for attention right there on our screens all hours of the day and the night. It is difficult for a person with even a modicum of conscience not to acknowledge that sorrow and slaughter are everywhere, that the most vulnerable human beings, women and children, especially, suffer degradations on a daily basis.

But does that mean we don't throw the Frisbee on the beach? That we don't delight in a meal eaten with friends in warm evening air or in the sight of the sun slipping into the ocean? Gilbert doesn't think so. He reminds us in this, a poem suffused with the savor of human dignity, that this world will always contain the full spectrum of human experience. All Gilbert's work seems to weave a fine thread between the classical and romantic attitudes to life. Staggering beauty and ravening pain live side by side in Nature. The summer dawn sheds light on the tiger's kill as well as its beauty. That's the way it is, so surely it must be what God wants.

You might say that God surely wants only the Good, and that we are the ones who deliver the evil—that it needn't be this way, that we can choose to live differently. But in that case, since God presumably made us with the faculty of choice, He/She must be willing to accept the results. And the results are not altogether commendable. Nor are they ever likely to be, for as the Buddha has said, suffering is intrinsic to the nature of this world. After all, shadowing every one of our moments, whether of ecstatic joy or profoundest sorrow, is the inevitable incursion of old age, sickness, and death. It is how we respond to suffering that makes all the difference, and Jack Gilbert is urging us to respond, despite everything, with an affirmation of life, which is joy.

The poor and the desperate know this better than anyone. For them, the specter of illness and deprivation is never far away. They know how precarious life is, and the resulting camaraderie of shared circumstance is perhaps one reason why they can laugh more easily than those of us who are buffered from life's exigencies by health insurance, clean running water, and purchasing power. Such buffers as these can lead us into either denial or guilt, and it is guilt that Jack Gilbert is urging us here to throw to the wind.

The women at the fountain know a woman is sick in the village. The old man in the gutter with hand outstretched doubles up in laughter at the quip of his friend. The prostitutes in their cages, there not by their own will, joke with one another like girls in the schoolyard. A sprawling shanty town on the edge of Calcutta is called the City of Joy. Somehow these people are closer to life's marrow than are we who are sheltered from life's harsher realities.

When there is nothing to lose, there is nothing to lose, and you can laugh more easily, especially when your lot is shared with others. Your laughter, far from denying or minimizing the pain, dignifies it. That is why nobility can be seen along with the suffering in refugee camps, in prison camps, and at death's door. In his poem "It's This Way," the Turkish dissident Nazim Hikmet, who spent more than twenty years in prison, says,

> *being captured is beside the point,*
> *the point is not to surrender.*[1]

Zainab Salbi, the remarkable young Iraqi woman who began the global nonprofit Women for Women, told me of the inspiration she received from being with women in Bosnia and also Rwanda who had been serially raped during the civil wars in those countries. These women were social outcasts. Although they had nothing and no one aside from one another, together they could see a future for themselves, and they refused to dwell in self-pity. From their perspective, there was no way left but up. They were full of life's possibilities, and Salbi found their laughter an inspiration.

We in the West are not the only ones with dreams. All those faces who fill our screens from the trouble spots of the world have their dreams, too; and because they are more keenly aware of the shadow in every moment, they are likely to be more pressingly awake to their dreams than we, who can so easily find every reason to put our dreams off till tomorrow. As Naomi Shihab Nye says in her poem "Kindness,"

> *Before you learn the tender gravity of kindness,*
> *you must travel where the Indian in a white poncho*
> *lies dead by the side of the road.*
> *You must see how this could be you,*
> *how he too was someone*
> *who journeyed through the night with plans . . .*[2]

Jack Gilbert goes on in this poem to say that

> *If we deny our happiness, resist our satisfaction,*
> *we lessen the importance of their deprivation.*

How can this be so? And why would we ever want to deny our own happiness? And yet we do. Think of the child—yourself, perhaps, long ago—who, full of glee at some new discovery, is told to be quiet by a parent; or worse, is told she was being foolish in making so much noise about something so trifling. We come to learn all too easily that if we raise our voice above the crowd, we lay ourselves open to ridicule, criticism, and the evil eye of plain old envy. And that can be enough to silence us for years. For a lifetime, even. We doubt ourselves, we doubt our own voice, our inspirations, the joy of our own creative urges—all for the sake of keeping the peace and preserving the mediocrity of the social norm. Wendell Berry says,

Why all the embarrassment
About being happy?[3]

Well, that's why: We fear the evil eye, the envious look that warns us we are stepping out of line, that we should be careful not to appear to be having a better time than those around us.

I come from a culture that, for all the dignity of its deep liberal values, does not like to see its own step too far out of line. The English are the masters of the put-down, delivered in a way that can seem incidental, harmless, but with results that can linger on for a lifetime. I love the country like an old friend who's been with me everywhere, but it's a tight little island, with little room to maneuver, so people get to know their place early, even if unconsciously and by inference. I always felt a little conspicuous in the English cultural landscape; I laughed too easily, and was generally too enthusiastic about most things that others felt lukewarm about. The English are a pragmatic people, and dreams, longings, and a penchant for the world of the spirit are best kept to oneself until you can show some concrete proof that they are likely to materialize. It is no accident, I believe, that I came to live in America, where there is more room to breathe and the possible is taken to be no less real than the actual.

So when Gilbert says,

We must risk delight

he is fully aware of the risk inherent in expressing delight. Take that risk, he urges. Be willing to stand out, make a noise, be different, to live in full abandon to the life that is rising inside you, no matter what anyone else around you might say.

Because of the lessons of self-restraint we have learned as a child, it is only natural that we might feel guilty about being happy when so many in the world are in pain. But Gilbert says here that if we deny our satisfaction, we actually lessen the importance of others' deprivation. How can that be?

I am inclined to ask the question this way: Does it help someone's pain to inflict pain on ourselves? To keep our head down, not to live as joyously as we have it in ourselves to do, is not compassion. Compassion is the expression of an awakened heart. But when we blunt our joy, we dull our hearts; we close them to the flood of life. That is why Jack Gilbert says that to close ourselves to joy diminishes the importance of the suffering of others—because we are also closing ourselves off from everyone else.

Another way we close ourselves off is through sheer indifference. W. H. Auden speaks to this in his famous poem "Musée des Beaux Arts," which was inspired by Breughel's painting *The Fall of Icarus*. There is Icarus, falling into the sea from his attempt to fly to the sun, while a ploughman, oblivious, keeps tilling the soil, and a ship sails on nonchalantly to some unknown destination. Suffering, Auden says, takes place

> *While someone else is eating or opening a window*
> *Or just walking dully along.*[4]

But this is not the response Gilbert is alluding to when he speaks of the poor women at the fountain laughing while someone in the village is very sick. I would like to think that their laughter, far from a sign of indifference, peals out *despite* the suffering they know. It is rather a sign of their stubbornness, their refusal to be cowed by their terrible circumstances. It is also the response called for by Rilke in so many of his poems. Rilke was convinced that the true role of a poet was to celebrate with praise the gift of life and the beauty of this world even in the midst of its suffering.

> *To praise is the whole thing,*[5]

he wrote. A compassionate intelligence knows this world is both heaven and hell, here and now, and is willing to feel the fullness of both ends of the spectrum as they arise. When we feel sorrow, our job is to feel the depths of the sorrow; when joy arises, to give ourselves to it utterly. Indifference is probably the greatest obstacle to this, the response of the awakened heart.

This world is a ruthless furnace, the poet says. It devours everything in its flames, and yet the flames are of two kinds, as Eliot reminds us:

> *The only hope, or else despair,*
> *Lies in the choice of pyre or pyre—*
> *To be redeemed by fire or fire.*[6]

The flames of hell or of the Holy Spirit surround our experience moment by moment. You do not have to be Christian to grasp Eliot's meaning; we make our own nest every second, and the difference between heaven and hell is no more than a hairsbreadth of attention. We "sink" into hell, into unconsciousness, or we "rise into heaven," into the clarity that can embrace everything, and the difference lies in our *stubbornness*—the act of will, or affirmation, required to accept and acknowledge our gladness when we feel it. Gladness has no place in the "hell" of self-absorption. It is expansive, turned outward to the world, rather than toward oneself alone.

Gilbert takes his stand even further in the next, almost shocking line:

> . . . *To make injustice the only*
> *measure of our attention is to praise the Devil.*

Our attention is our gift to the world. It is in effect our means of blessing whatever it is we give it to, which is why a child who has not been given sufficient attention does not feel blessed. If we give our attention solely to evil in its various guises, then yes, in this way we are praising the Devil, because that is all we can see. Perhaps it is for this reason that so many social activists suffer from burnout. It must become pretty exhausting to see the world only in shades of struggle and injustice.

> *If the locomotive of the Lord runs us down,*
> *we should give thanks that the end had magnitude.*

Whatever shape or form it comes in—a sudden illness, perhaps, the loss of a job—that locomotive will indeed run us down in the long run, one way or another. For this line hints at the unexpected more than at death from natural causes, something roaring out of a tunnel we never knew even existed. In a powerful poem called "Things Ended," the Greek poet C. P. Cavafy speaks to how we so often

> *. . . plan how to avoid the inevitable*
> *danger that threatens us so terribly.*[7]

Then he says we discover—too late—that the danger we were anticipating is not the one that's coming at all, and that suddenly,

> *Another disaster, one we never imagined,*
> *. . . sweeps us away.*

The unexpected always blows open a space in our mind, usually so full of preconceptions and expectations. And we might say that in such moments of sudden clarity, everything is brought into sharp relief and amplified, which is why such a moment has magnitude.

We must admit there will be music despite everything.

The people of Sarajevo were encouraged to admit this when the city was surrounded by Serbs and sniper fire could kill them while standing in the bread line or collecting a child from school. Some of the city orchestra brought their instruments into the town square and played day after day for hours in defiance of the madness of war. Their music symbolized the indestructibility of the human spirit despite everything.

The last, lucid image of this poem probably came from Jack Gilbert's long experience of living on Santorini, a magical Greek island in the Aegean. Soon after his first volume of poetry was published to great acclaim in 1962 (which—in no small part owing to his remarkably good looks—got him, improbably for a poet, on the front page of *Esquire,* and even in *Teen Magazine*), Gilbert left the promise of literary fame and fortune in America to roam around Europe on a Guggenheim Fellowship. Choosing a deliberate and radical cultivation of solitude over the easy allure of celebrity at home, Gilbert was away for twenty years or more, much of it on Santorini. He disappeared from the literary scene, and *Refusing Heaven,* the recent collection that includes "A Brief for the Defense," is only his fourth book in eighty years.

I myself remember arriving just before dawn in the crescent bay of Santorini in 1965, somewhat queasy from the journey from Crete in an old boat that had groaned its way all through the night, overloaded with goats and people and chickens. I remember, too, the oars of the small boats as they rowed out in the dark to pick us up in handfuls and take us to shore, where braying donkeys were waiting to jog us up the steep cliffs to the tiny settlement above.

For Gilbert, the sound of those oars is worth all the years of sorrow that are to come. In a radio interview, he once told how he had almost always been happy in his life—mostly poor and cold, sometimes scared, but always in delight at the privilege of being allowed to breathe, to see, to feel, to smell, to love. And to hear the faint sound of oars. Gilbert's poetry—and this poem as much as any he ever wrote—reveals a deep conviction that transcendence is possible in this world, despite the crushing forces of cynicism that are everywhere. One moment of full attention is one moment fully lived, and Gilbert never lets us forget in this wonderful poem that this is a privilege always available to us, a privilege that can lead to true delight.

7

WHAT TO REMEMBER
WHEN WAKING

by David Whyte

In that first
hardly noticed
moment
in which you wake,
coming back
to this life
from the other
more secret,
moveable
and frighteningly
honest
world
where everything
began,
there is a small
opening
into the day
which closes
the moment

you begin
your plans.

What you can plan
is too small
for you to live.

What you can live
wholeheartedly
will make plans
enough
for the vitality
hidden in your sleep.

To be human
is to become visible
while carrying
what is hidden
as a gift to others.

To remember
the other world
in this world
is to live in your
true inheritance.

You are not
a troubled guest
on this earth,
you are not
an accident
amidst other accidents
you were invited
from another and greater
night
than the one
from which
you have just emerged.

Now, looking through
the slanting light
of the morning
window toward
the mountain
presence
of everything
that can be,
what urgency
calls you to your
one love? What shape
waits in the seed
of you to grow

and spread
its branches
against a future sky?

Is it waiting
in the fertile sea?
In the trees
beyond the house?
In the life
you can imagine
for yourself?
In the open
and lovely
white page
on the waiting desk?

your true inheritance

Any moment can take us by surprise, if we are open to surprises. Yet in the moment we first open our eyes in the morning, there is a window, a brief opening when the world can be seen fresh and new without the stream of opinions and ideas that kick in a moment later about everything we have to do when we get up.

In that brief interlude, the world we have just emerged from lingers still in our senses; the dream, the savor, the feel of it seeps into that first moment when we open our eyes onto this more concrete world of tangible sights and sounds and substances. David Whyte calls it the

> *more secret,*
> *moveable*
> *and frighteningly*
> *honest*
> *world*
> *where everything*
> *began, . . .*

Now why does Whyte say that the world we have just awoken from is more honest? More frighteningly honest, even?

I suspect it is because in the subtle world of sleep nothing is bound by our preconceptions about how things are meant to be; the brakes are off, and images appear free of the constraints and opinions of the conscious mind. Reality there is neither defined nor confined by strategic or forward thinking. The one who has gone to sleep is the very one who normally censors our daylight thinking and feeling and who tailors our behavior to fit the public image of ourselves we feel most comfortable with.

So in our sleep we are more honest with ourselves, whether we wish it or not. And that can be scary because we might not like all that we see, and we no longer have the capacity to cut and paste our experience according to our preferences. In the sleep world, we get what we get and it won't always be pretty. But it will always be honest, and sometimes frighteningly so. After all, who would ever want to be jumping off a cliff or be engulfed in a tidal wave, for example; or killing a deer on the road? If we can only read the symbols, our deeper layers of thinking and feeling are revealed in the darkness of night.

When we wake into our plans, not just for the day but for ourselves, we narrow the nightlife stream down to the tiniest trickle. We are bigger than our plans, Whyte says in this poem, and we serve that bigger life when we carry over some of the vitality of our night vision into the day. Strange thought, that our sleep holds more vitality than our waking hours! And yet it's another kind of vitality Whyte is speaking to here: the vitality you might associate with a great ocean rather than with that of a boxer, or of someone who successfully ploughs through their to-do list day after day. The *vitality / hidden in your sleep* is a deep well with a source far beyond the layers of your personal experience of struggle, of loss and gain, hope and fear. Its source is the ocean, the teeming web of life that sustains all things. That sort of vitality is endless, because it doesn't belong to us and is not generated by the personal will. But it is what lives and moves through everything we think and do, whether we know it or not.

The way to be in touch with that living stream during the day, says Whyte, is to live wholeheartedly. When we are no longer separated into the doer and the observer, when part of us is no longer hanging back on the sidelines of our experience, uncertain whether this is what we really want or not, when we are wholly immersed in our life, the stream that waters the night will start flowing into our day. To live wholeheartedly doesn't necessarily imply we should be engaged in furious activity. It means that we follow the thread of what we are doing, whatever we are doing, moment to moment. When we are immersed in a process like this, whether it be serving dinner or running a business or resting on the sofa, the personal will falls subservient to the current, to the flow, that is inherent in the activity itself.

A few moments ago I was wholeheartedly spread on the sofa, in the middle of the day, with not even the smallest hankering to be somewhere else. Lying there in that wholehearted way—giving the weight not only of my body but also of my mind to the soft velvet cushions beneath me—it dawned on me that my life at this time is doing precisely what David Whyte speaks of here; it is giving space to the vitality hidden inside me. For the first time in several years, I have no plans for another book when I have finished this one. I have no plans for the future at all, other than to go to Europe for a couple of months this summer. I did suggest writing a book on the subject of food and the way of life that surrounds it in Europe, but my publisher was not sufficiently impressed by the idea to want to finance a jaunt around the Mediterranean.

It interested me that this turn of events caused barely a ripple in my peace of mind. In fact, something in me relaxed. I could feel my life opening up around me and beyond me, bigger than me and my plans. I realized I would go to Europe anyway, not least because, after nine years or so in America, it is time for me to feel my belonging in Europe again, but also because I could sense that some deeper core that I don't quite know the name of yet needs to be unearthed. Perhaps some piece of writing is asking to be done, some theme wanting to be revealed, like a vein in rock, that strikes to the core of my own story more than any book I could have written on food. This small realization, I like to think, is an expression of the vitality in this poem. Not the vitality of effort—which wins races, gets things done, and generally makes the world go round—but of the relaxed state of mind that welcomes the rippling vitality of being, and the way it reveals our path step by step, rather than through the long view.

> *To be human*
> *is to become visible*
> *while carrying*

what is hidden
as a gift to others.

We become truly visible only when we give voice to that which is hidden in us. And what is hidden is the rare gem, our uniqueness, the essence of who we are, the greatest gift we have to offer anyone, which is never absent in the darkness when we sleep. I would like to think that the essence of who I am will be the source of my next breath, my next years, my next book, if indeed there is to be one. Wouldn't that be the richest of lives?

To remember
the other world
in this world
is to live in your
true inheritance.

Every spiritual tradition speaks of remembrance, and of its twin, forgetting. "Remember me," the old song goes. Remember where you came from, which was not from this world. The Sufis tell the story of the prince who was given away to peasants to raise, and who forgot his true inheritance, only to be awoken to it years later by an emissary from his father. The themes of waking and sleeping are further echoes of remembering and forgetting. But in this poem, Whyte turns the worlds upside down. It seems we are most awake when asleep. In our normal waking state, we forget our true inheritance—which is why he urges us to feel the thread of the *other world* even as we move and speak in this one.

Remember, not in the sense of a memory to be recalled whenever you think of it, but as a felt sense of your own marrow, an embodied sense of the depths you came from and that, even now, you are joined to. Those depths are the source of your living spirit in this moment, and they are not elsewhere, in some heavenly realm, but here, just beneath your skin, breathing you moment by moment. This is why many traditions employ bodily prayer practices, and why it is often recommended to feel the sensation of your right hand, or some other part of your body, while you are speaking or walking or going about your business. Not constantly—that would be the equivalent of unceasing prayer, a formidable practice—but for fifteen minutes, say, several times a day. This is why Muslims pray five times a day, kneeling and bowing their head low to the ground each time; and why many religions have their equivalent of the rosary. The remembrance, anchored in the body.

When we remember even faintly who we are in this way and what we are joined to, the more usual identity of a *troubled guest* or *an accident / amidst other accidents* falls away. The troubled guest is the seeker who feels lost, without a guide, and when we are a guest, we are away from home. We are separate from all we hold dear. But at least the seeker has an intimation of home, of some other way, some other possibility, even if he cannot quite reach it or feel it within his grasp.

Those who feel they are accidents among other accidents do not even have that consolation. They are the atheists, the materialists, the existentialists for whom everything is the mere play of random chance and the only meaning lies in the acceptance of meaninglessness. We probably all feel like this at one time or another, but it must take a rare form of courage to live as if your very existence was an accident, the courage to live without hope, without any other reality than that which you can see with your physical eyes. It must also take a refusal to see what lives in the night.

Don't get confused by some mistaken identity, Whyte says. We are neither an accident nor a troubled guest, even though it may sometimes or indeed often feel like it. But now Whyte points to a darker and deeper night than the one we awoke from this morning. As if to say that our night vision and the uncensored world beneath our eyelids is only a harbinger, or metaphor perhaps, for something much more vast and inky than we can ever imagine. A black hole, some endless reach of dark matter, which is not only the center of the universe but also the source of our mind; and perhaps the two are one and the same. You and I, the poet says, were invited from out of that dark and fathomless space into this life we are living now. And we come trailing starlight, whether we know it or not.

Given this, waking up into our day to behold once again— or for the first time—the tangible presence of this world of mountains and slanting light and breakfast and clothes to put on and perhaps children to attend to, given all this,

> *what urgency*
> *calls you to your*
> *one love?*

Urgency, not as in someone who is late for work; not as in desperation, the hurry to get something over with, no. Rather, the urgency of a seed to become a flower or a tree. The seed is bursting with the sense, the intimation, of its own destiny, purpose, with the whole point of being a seed. It can't see the oak tree within it; it can't even name it or give any sensible description of it. But it can feel it. It is that something that is pressing against its outer skin. It both wants it to happen, to burst forth into blossom, and allows it to happen. When the small will and the greater will are joined, the blossoming can spring forth. And at the very same time that the seed is sensing the oak tree, the oak tree is calling to the seed. Our fullness, our deep wholeness as individuals, is already present in embryo. It calls to us, sings to us the song we were born for, urging us to grow into what we may become.

The blossoming is our one love; it is what we were born for, whatever shape or form that it may have for us personally. Perhaps it is waiting still in the *fertile sea*, the unconscious, the crucible that spawns our unknown futures, still as yet beyond our conscious grasp. Perhaps it is already formed and in this world, a slot or a niche just waiting for you to fill it, just a little beyond where you can see from your window. Or perhaps the blossoming has already begun in the form of images in your imagination, or vague presentiments that words have not yet quite put into sentences.

On the other hand, perhaps your one love is a creative love, a song or a dance or a poem or a novel or (in my case) an essay like this one that is waiting, pregnant, to fill the white page. For me, the white page is literal. The white page offers me a cup for *the more secret, / moveable / and frighteningly / honest / world* that wants to find its way through my fingers onto that whiteness. And I don't know, I don't know, what is going to come out of my mouth or out of my fingers onto that whiteness. Nor can I know how honest it will be, usually not until sometime later, when the words have dried and I can begin to see them with a certain distance. As for the not knowing, that is the richness, the trembling, of it all. The white page will always be bigger than I am, willing and able to contain more than I could ever dream of putting into words.

The white page is not just for writers. The literal page is just one more metaphor for that infinite canvas ready to be condensed and shaped into the story of a human life—one particular human life, yours perhaps, or mine. Pour yourself like a fountain onto the page, Whyte suggests. He is speaking to everyone who still has a blank page left to fill in his life, which is to say anyone who still has a future. Which is to say anyone who is alive. What is it that Mary Oliver said? I remember, I remember, I remember. She said:

> . . . *what is it you plan to do*
> *with your one wild and precious life?*[1]

8

WITH THAT MOON LANGUAGE

by Hafiz

Admit something:

Everyone you see, you say to them, "Love me."
Of course you do not do this out loud; otherwise,
*   someone would call the cops.*
Still, though, think about this, this great pull in us
*   to connect.*
Why not become the one who lives with a full moon
*   in each eye that is always saying,*
with that sweet moon language,
what every other eye in this world is dying to hear?

(translated by Daniel Ladinsky)

call the cops

Hafiz, we've heard this all before, though usually in reference to someone else; and certainly in more subtle, more psychologically nuanced language. Why do you have to be so direct? So sharp? So unequivocal?

Everyone you see, you say to them, "Love me."

You mean me? You mean that *I* walk around all day with a big sign on my chest saying LOVE ME? I don't see myself that way. Not me. Though I do understand that there are many people in that sad situation; and I would even go so far as to admit that we may all, from time to time, suffer a little from the condition. But surely there are degrees of the ailment, from high fever to a barely discernible tone of voice or look in the eyes?

This is why Hafiz has to be sharp. His words need to cut like a knife through our defenses to get to the core of the truth. No one wants to hear this. It's embarrassing. It's humbling. But the cleaner the wound, the quicker it heals. And the truth is, however self-determining we may take ourselves to be, however mature and at home with ourselves we may feel, it is still likely that, in the wings of our awareness, there is some little person in us who never quite grew up, who is always waiting for the slightest opportunity to squeeze some acknowledgment from his parents, whatever shape or form they may assume in his adult life.

So we want to be loved. Of course we do. And one of the most common ways we have of feeling that feeling is to gain the approval of others. No doubt this contributes to our need to build the tallest skyscraper, run the fastest mile, deliver the best speech, write the best book. There are other, far more significant contributing factors to human achievement, of course—the urgency of a talent or deeply felt conviction to express itself, for example; or the upwelling of a fountain of creativity from *the deep heart's core,* to borrow a phrase from Yeats. To say otherwise would be sheer reductionism, a diminishment of the human spirit. And yet this need for approval, which we take to be love, can so easily seep into everything we say and do.

We want to prove ourselves; yes, for our own satisfaction, but also to our father, or maybe our mother, and to our peers. We want to be recognized, esteemed, and valued, a perfectly natural and valid desire. Yet so easily, we can look for that recognition in all the wrong places. Sometimes for years, sometimes for a lifetime, we may tailor our behavior to fit the image of what we think others will want and like. We conform socially, we do all the right things, maybe we even go to the school or take up the course of study our father always wanted us to, the profession that he, perhaps, took up himself. Or we rebel, and do the opposite, which amounts to the same thing: We are still at the effect of our need to be loved.

Maybe we manage to sort out the issue by our thirties, or maybe our forties. Maybe we manage to begin creating a life that is more genuinely our own, rather than one made according to the image of others, and of the collective norm. Even so, we still need to be liked, respected. I know a woman who is a successful model. She has felt ambivalent about her job for years. But she finds it very difficult—impossible, thus far—to leave. It's not just the money or the travel—those attractions palled a while ago. I suspect she gets something else that would be difficult for most people to give up. She gets admiration; she gets the constant affirmation that she is not only beautiful, but that she does her work well. She feels valued, and that is a healthy and empowering feeling.

The only trouble is, we all know in our hearts that the approval of others for our achievements, our beauty, even the nobility of our character, is not enough, however gratifying it may be. It is not yet the love that we are really looking for, which is why we can feel hollow even in the midst of our greatest successes. In fact, our own inner emptiness can seem all the more gaping and impossible to fill when we receive public acclaim and honor, yet still feel something lacking inside. I will never forget a famous speaker telling me that the times he most dreaded, the times he felt most painfully alone, were when he opened the door to his hotel room after having left the stage and a thousand people applauding him. He is not the first performer to admit that he only really feels filled up, full of life, loved, when he is on stage. But it doesn't last, and it can't. Because it is not the love he is really looking for. It is not what any of us are really looking for.

Looking for love in all the wrong places is something we have all done at one time or another. Many of us spend our entire lives doing it. Many relationships are doomed because of it. Even so,

Of course you do not do this out loud . . .

says Hafiz. I take this to mean that we don't acknowledge openly to the people in our lives that we want them to love us—in the sense of filling us up somehow, making us happy, giving our lives meaning—and that we don't even say the truth out loud to ourselves. In fact, we are likely to deny to our family and friends, and also to ourselves, that any such thing is happening, that we would ever dream of expecting someone else to make us happy. We are perfectly capable of doing that ourselves, thank you very much. Except, it seems, we are not. And, either in words or in action, we can even blame those around us for not giving us what we secretly expect is our due from them!

Hafiz, being a Sufi, is always singing about love. But he does not mean the kind of "love" the "wanting creature" inside of us is looking for. That kind of love is a need, the kind that cries out, "Love me." The kind of love that interests Hafiz is that which can only begin when the wanting ceases.

Still, though, think about this, this great pull
in us to connect.

It is the most natural thing in the world to want to love and be loved, Hafiz acknowledges. In our natural, healthy state, we like to touch and be touched, to feel the warmth of another's body, to roll in the grass. We want to connect to others. But not only in that simple, warm, and affectionate way of the body, which in itself can be so nourishing. We also want to connect beneath words, beneath our skin, through the eyes of the heart. We want to know the taste of loving and being loved in our essence, for who we are.

Here, though, is the rub. How do we go about it? How do we invite the experience of a love that is not merely a need? All spiritual traditions have urged us to love one another. We tend to assume that this is the message of only the New rather than the Old Testament, but there it is in Leviticus 19:18: *Thou shalt love thy neighbor as thyself.* Here it is in a poem by Hafiz the Sufi. Loving-kindness is central to the teaching of Mahayana Buddhism, too. These teachings have been around for a few thousand years, and yet is the world a more loving place now than it ever was? There is not a great deal of evidence to suggest there has been much improvement. And if improvement there be, it is mostly due to the teachings of the European and American Enlightenment, with its ideas of universal suffrage, equality, freedom, and a gradually developing respect for those human beings and also forms of life that are different from ourselves.

In this poem, Hafiz is urging us to express our love to those around us rather than to expect to receive it from them. Give the very thing you are looking for.

Why not become the one who lives with a full moon
　　in each eye that is always saying,
with that sweet moon language,
what every other eye in this world is dying to hear?

But Hafiz begs the question, Why don't we do what we know we should do? Why do we, even if only subtly, go on searching and wanting, rather than giving? The philosopher Jacob Needleman gives his whole attention to this question in his book *Why Can't We Be Good?*[1] He quotes St. Paul, who cries out: "The good that I would, that I do not; but the evil which I would not, that I do."[2] Paul is making it clear that, despite his best intentions, he is *unable* to do the good he wishes. In the same way, if we look and are honest with ourselves, we must acknowledge that we, too, are unable to love the people in our world in the way that we know we ought. I don't mean just your marriage partner. I mean the woman at the checkout counter who is taking her time with the lady in front of you. I mean the man who has just taken the parking place you were eyeing, or the tech-support guy in Bombay who doesn't seem to understand your accent. I mean the world we live in, with all its imperfections. It's easy enough to feel loving and open when the person concerned is showing us genuine respect and concern, or generosity, or understanding. But the world isn't always like that, or even often like that.

So, in the face of the way things are, why can't we say

what every other eye in this world is dying to hear?

Why can't we just get on and do what Jesus said, love one another? Needleman quotes a saying of Hillel the Elder, the great rabbinic patriarch, as a key to this question:

> *If I am not for myself, who will be for me?*
> *And if I am for myself alone, what am I?*
> *And if not now, when?*

Before we consider Hillel's statement, let's first remember that we live in a very different age (with very different notions of what it means to be human) from the time of Hillel, who was alive in the time of King Herod. The current fashion for atheism—in the form of Richard Dawkins's scientism, or Christopher Hitchens's personal brand in his book *God Is Not Great,* or Sam Harris's *The End of Faith*—assumes that human nature is essentially materialist and selfish, and has no purpose beyond itself. And there is a great deal to substantiate this view, not only in the world in general, but within the history and the continuing power structures of religions themselves. At the other end of the spectrum, we have the expansion of fundamentalism, with its insistence on a literal understanding of scripture, and on the authority of received belief instead of any self-examination or questioning.

Yet throughout history, all the great spiritual traditions, along with philosophers including Socrates and Plato and poets and lovers of God such as Hafiz, Rumi, Kabir, and countless others, have shared a view of the human being very different from either of these two current trends. Despite our history and the evidence around us to the contrary, there is in the individual a quality that reaches beyond his personal concerns and that can stand in some way as a loving witness to the events of his life, both in it and outside of it at the same time. This unique human quality, this view maintains, becomes available, not through hearsay or through a belief in it, but through a personal and interior intention. This witness is our gateway to freedom and love.

In the Upanishads, human consciousness is represented by two birds, one looking on while the other drinks at a fountain. When we are able to step back from the opinions and beliefs, the moods and emotions of our ordinary self, and bear witness in this way, we are in the orbit of the soul, or the Self. And in that orbit, we are aware of the presence of something higher, something far beyond ourselves. And we bow down.

You can see the same image, two birds at a fountain, one looking on while the other drinks, in Byzantine art. I remember gazing up at it in amazement in a fifth-century church in Ravenna, Italy. It is a universal insight into human nature, a lived experience on the part of countless people all over the world throughout time. In this view, one must first be able to sort the wheat from the chaff in oneself, the small self from the big Self, in order to be able to love. The personality—the opinions, drives, desires, and needs we usually identify with—cannot love. It can only want. And as long as we know ourselves only as our daily bundle of thoughts and feelings, we will continue to wear that sign around our neck: LOVE ME.

So Needleman suggests that when Hillel says the first task is to be for oneself, he means that we must feel our way to the Self that is veiled by the personality. No one else can do that for us. And when we stand in and as the Self, we are automatically aware of our connection with everyone and everything. When we are for ourselves alone, we are imprisoned in the personality. We cannot see or feel our connection with anyone or anything beyond ourselves. Then, says Hillel, imprisoned in this way, *What am I?*

In the Self, we are also aware that we stand under and are illumined by the power of something much greater than ourselves, which is the ultimate source of any love we might feel. The theistic traditions personalize this something and call it God. In Buddhism, it is equivalent to Great Space, or Spaciousness. This is why the first commandment is to love your God with all your might, and then the second is to love your neighbor as yourself. Love is not ultimately ours to give; it is a gift from God, from Creation, that moves through us as we stand in its light.

The personality cannot really love anything, though it can have a lot of firm opinions about love. When we edge back from our habitual identity, into the orbit of the Self, we become open to the love of God. With at least an intuition of that love—the love that makes the world go round—we naturally begin to *be* that love, to express it in our lives just by the way we are. We begin to be able to love our neighbor. Not only that, but we can begin to love our own human nature, with all its flaws and imperfections. It's not a matter of getting rid of our imperfections, but of not being dictated to by them. When we can love our own humanity just as it is, we can love the human frailty of others, too.

But Hafiz, or Hillel for that matter, is not recommending the usual pop psychology approach of "love yourself": Give yourself a bubble bath, a massage, some positive affirmations before you go to bed at night. Those are all well and good, but they are the personality talking to itself, trying to fix itself. And it will never succeed. We might feel better about ourselves for a while, but feeling better is not what we are talking about here. In fact, stepping back, or rather falling back and bearing witness, may not be comfortable. It may engender remorse for what one sees in one's ordinary way of going about living—the way we judge others, perhaps; or the way we try and feel better about ourselves by diminishing someone else. Remorse is good medicine. It helps us see ourselves as we are, without guilt or shame, but with an honest gaze that can come only from another dimension or level in ourselves. And it was Plato, among many others, and for want of a better name, who called that other dimension the Self.

So Hafiz, lover of God that he is, in his cryptic question *Why not become . . .* is urging us by implication to take these steps—back into ourselves and out toward others, both steps being predicated on what for him is a love of God so wild he falls down drunk with it most days. Imagine what a grace it would be if one day, this day maybe, like Hafiz, we were able to mumble through trembling lips, what everyone we meet wants to hear.

9

AWAKEN AS THE BELOVED
by St. Symeon the Theologian

We awaken in Christ's body
as Christ awakens our bodies,
and my poor hand is Christ, He enters
my foot, and is infinitely me.

I move my hand, and wonderfully
my hand becomes Christ, becomes all of Him
(for God is indivisibly
whole, seamless in His Godhood).

I move my foot, and at once
he appears like a flash of lightning.
Do my words seem blasphemous?—Then
open your heart to Him

and let yourself receive the one
who is opening to you so deeply.
For if we genuinely love Him,
we wake up inside Christ's body

where all our body, all over,
every most hidden part of it,
is realized in joy as Him,
and He makes us, utterly, real,

and everything that is hurt, everything
that seemed to us dark, harsh, shameful,
maimed, ugly, irreparably
damaged, is in Him transformed

and recognized as whole, as lovely,
as radiant in His light
we awaken as the Beloved
in every last part of our body.

(translated by Stephen Mitchell)

every last part of our body

To fully appreciate this remarkable poem, it helps to read it in context, in the context of tenth-century Byzantium, of early Christian mysticism, and of the universal insights of the mystical tradition everywhere. Perhaps, I don't know, but perhaps you will start reading this poem and find its Christian framework something of a hurdle. Perhaps, like me, you were born into a Christian culture, have absorbed Christian language and imagery like the air, but have never been attracted to church religion or dogma, or even to the notion of Christ as savior. By the time I read to the end of this poem, however, it was obvious to me that this was not another hymn from my Anglican childhood. By the last line, I realized I was being given a glimpse of a vision and quality of feeling that is universal, that is earth-shattering in its implications, and that also exists in our own Western tradition.

The ecstasy and realization that St. Symeon declares here is clothed by every culture in its own language, and has been celebrated in different ways all across the world. If you replace the word *Christ* in this poem by either *Him* or *That,* or even *the Tao,* you would have something that could come equally from the Hindu Upanishads, from China, or from any number of

Sufi teachers. But the word is *Christ*, and I am glad, because Symeon is showing us a wisdom here in our own Christian tradition—significantly, though, from the Eastern Orthodox tradition rather than from the Latin or Protestant churches—that many, including I, have looked for in other religions altogether.

St. Symeon could almost be called the Rumi of the Greek Orthodox Church, and this is a Rumi poem in Christian language. Symeon lived a couple of hundred years before the great Sufi saint, in what is now the same country, Turkey. He was born in 949 in Paphlagonia, in northern Turkey, into a Byzantine family of provincial nobles, at a time when the Byzantine Empire was once again at its height of influence and power across the whole Eastern Mediterranean. The tenth century saw Byzantium spread its Orthodox faith into Russia and the Baltics, and recover Anatolia and Syria from the Muslims. In the following century, the Seljuk Turks regained Anatolia, and much more besides, which is why Rumi lived and taught there, in the city of Konya. In the tenth century, though, Orthodox Christianity was in full revival, and monasteries sprang up all over the empire, especially around the area of Mount Athos, in northern Greece, which is still under the jurisdiction of the Patriarch of Constantinople, rather than that of the Greek government.

At the age of fourteen, Symeon finished his secondary education at the court of the two brother emperors, Basil and Constantine, in Constantinople (today's Istanbul). He met his spiritual father there, St. Symeon the Studite, and though the young man begged to be allowed to enter the famous monastery of Studion, he was made to wait until he was twenty-seven years old—a classic spiritual teaching in itself. During that long period, Symeon was busy in the world, probably as a diplomat for the court, while spending his evenings in night vigils and reading spiritual works. One of his elder's advice to him during that time was "If you desire to have always a soul-saving guidance, pay heed to your conscience and without fail do what it will instill in you." Conscience, in the language of the early Desert Fathers, had nothing to do with guilt. It meant the Self, or soul, the one in us that knows.

However, within several months of achieving his long-held desire of joining the monastery, Symeon was thrown out on his ear! He was too passionate for the community, which, like many monasteries at the time, had an intellectual approach to theology. Symeon, as this poem clearly shows, was all for a personal experience of the divine. He was for immanence, whereas the religious climate in Constantinople was dominated by the abstract, scholastic theory of Archbishop Nicodemia, the official court theologian.

The same schism was to play out for centuries between the Roman and Orthodox churches—with Latin, Western culture being profoundly influenced by the intellectual rigor and scholasticism of Thomas Aquinas while the Orthodox were influenced by the monks on Mount Athos and by the writings of St. Symeon. The Orthodox eventually came down firmly on the side of the mystics who claimed to have had a personal experience of God, and, as in this poem, even to be indistinguishable from God. Symeon urged his monks to return to the spirit of the early church, in which personal realization was held to be more important than the outward form of church dogma and life. The mystical element of Orthodox Christianity, known as hesychasm (quietism) remains a powerful force even today; in the monasteries of Mount Athos, the works of Symeon are still read as a matter of course and his methods are put into practice.

Symeon went off into a remote region toward the east and revived an ailing monastic community there; he began in the course of time to be the first main influence in Orthodoxy to give validity and credence to the mystical way. For him, wisdom was infused by the Holy Spirit rather than learned in books, and its supreme expression was the knowledge of the overwhelming divine light of God that blinds the eyes of the soul. Using the word *intellect* much as we would the term *mindfulness,* or *attention,* Symeon says, in "The Three Methods of Prayer,"

Search inside yourself with your intellect so as to find the place of the heart, where all the powers of the soul reside. To start with you will find there darkness and an impenetrable density. Later you will find as though miraculously an unceasing joy. For as soon as intellect attains the place of the heart, at once it sees things of which it previously knew nothing. It sees the open space within the heart and it beholds it entirely luminous and full of discrimination. From then on, from whatever side a distractive thought may appear, before it has come to a completion and assumed a form, the in-

tellect immediately drives it away and destroys it
with the invocation of Jesus Christ. . . . the rest you
will learn for yourself.[1]

This mystical realization was reached by ascetic practices
of solitude, bodily stillness, and prayer, in particular the Jesus
Prayer, which involved the repetition of the name Jesus coor-
dinated with the breath. The name was brought down on the
breath into the heart, and the aim was to eventually have the
prayer "say itself" naturally and unceasingly. The practice was
transmitted by the early Fathers of the Sinai Desert to Byzan-
tine monks, though its origins are in the spiritual exercises
of the Pythagorean Greeks and the Alexandrian Gnostics, as
well as the ancient Jews. Later, the Sufis of the Muslim terri-
tories to the east of Byzantium developed similar techniques
with the breath and the name of Allah.

Some thirty years ago I was moved by the writings and
especially the presence of Archbishop Anthony of Sourozh,
head of the Russian Church in London and also in Western
Europe, to attend the long Russian mass regularly and to
seek his spiritual guidance. I will never forget him telling me,
one day in a quiet corner at the back of the church, that the
essence of Christianity is obedience; and that obedience, in
its original sense, meant listening. I took up the Prayer of the
Heart for a while, but I was unable to overcome my lack of
feeling for the name of Jesus. I suppose I couldn't listen
deeply enough. I felt a fraud, somehow, because I seemed to
be calling on someone I didn't feel love for. My god was
nameless, and has remained so till this day. A year or so after

our first meeting, the archbishop sent me a postcard of an image of the Buddha. I wasn't a Buddhist, and am not one now; but we both knew what his card meant. Though we parted, his influence on my life, his impersonal yet intimate presence, remains with me as ever.

Symeon's poem begins with these lines:

> *We awaken in Christ's body*
> *as Christ awakens our bodies, . . .*

This is the whole point of the mystic's life, whatever religion he may profess: to awaken. To awaken from the dream of feeling separate from God and from all that is, into the realization of the unity of all things. For Symeon, this means to awaken into the realization that everything is Christ's body, and as we realize this, he says, our own bodies are awakened cell by cell. We are literally transfigured in that awareness. This, then, is the true resurrection, here on earth, now. Not that we walk around like pillars of light, but that the awareness of the truth is itself the light that makes everything look and feel different, even though everything is exactly as it always was. Nothing has changed except for the one who is looking.

The saint's *poor hand,* his foot, every part of him is filled with the infinite that he calls Christ; and since God is *indivisibly whole, seamless,* there is nowhere that he begins and God ends. The whole of creation is seamless, of a piece, which means that there is nothing that does not partake in God, that there is nowhere that God is not. Everything, then, not just the individual known as Symeon, is God shining. The Latin Church rejected this teaching loudly, because for them it smacked of pantheism and the old pagan religions. The West would have to wait for the arrival of the Romantic poets in the eighteenth century to hear this view spoken freely again.

Symeon is well aware that his words *seem blasphemous.* After all, who dares to equate themselves with Christ? The only way to understand Symeon is to

open your heart to Him

and let yourself receive the one
who is opening to you so deeply.

We will each have our own language for opening the heart, but Symeon is a Christian, so for him the foundation for such an opening is baptism, the guidance of a spiritual father, unceasing prayer, and also the practice of repentance. Baptism is the gateway to entering the Christian family, so it is not surprising that Symeon sees this to be the first step. It is the beginning, however, not the end, of the Orthodox way of transformation; it's not a matter of getting dunked and becoming reborn. Unlike some contemporary Christian evangelicals or charismatics, Symeon's unitive view is not a more emotional than conceptual one. It is the result of serious practices sustained by deep faith, a faith that relies not on outer creeds but on both the spiritual authority of a guide (a universal requirement among mystics) and a personal longing for God.

Repentance is not a popular word today; it comes trailing odors of sinfulness and wrongdoing, and much of the popular psychology of the past thirty years has been concerned, rightly so, with restoring a positive self-image in place of the guilt and self-loathing that the Catholic Church in particular has done much to encourage over the last thousand years. But the original Greek word *metanoia* means to "turn around." It means a turning of the heart toward God. It's not about self-loathing or shame; it's about acknowledging—seeing, in a felt way—how we have made ourselves separate from Him, and in the acknowledgment, returning our attention toward Him. Again, the heart for the mystic is not an emotional, so much as a feeling organ, and the difference is palpable.

The early Greek mystics spoke of the need for *apatheia,* which literally means "without emotions," when entering a state of contemplation or deep prayer. Our word *apathy* is derived from this Greek term, but the meaning of the original was very different. It meant something more like equanimity, or a peaceful attentiveness. The fourth-century mystic Evagrius wrote that "this *apatheia* has a child called *agape* [love of God] who keeps the door to deep knowledge of the created universe. Finally, to this knowledge succeed theology and the supreme beatitude."[2] The love of God, then, is not an emotion. It is a reality that arises in deep presence, when the inner eye of the heart is open and sees clearly. From this alone true theology arises, says Evagrius—rather than from intellectual argument or debate. And from this alone emerges the "supreme beatitude," the unitive vision that Symeon praises.

Symeon places the emphasis in this poem less on reaching

out to Christ than on receiving the love that is always there.
Yet who is loving whom? I wonder. Perhaps it is Christ Him-
self's love that pours through us and back to Him and back
again. Perhaps to *genuinely love Him* means simply to recog-
nize His preexistent love for us. In the opening heart—not
an emotion, remember, but rather a presence—the indivis-
ible stream can flow, and any difference between who we
think ourselves to be and who we imagine Christ to be disap-
pears. Then

> . . . *all our body, all over,*
> *every most hidden part of it,*
> *is realized in joy as Him,* . . .

The realization takes place throughout the entire physical
being—not in the mind or even in the heart alone. This
seems to me the most beautiful affirmation of the physical
world, so unusual in the more canonical Christian texts and
yet so resonant with the Christian promise of broken bodies
being made whole, of the transfiguration of Christ. Except the
transfiguration that Symeon speaks of takes place here and
now—not in the historical time of Jesus, nor on some future
Judgment Day—for any individual who is able to *genuinely
love Him*. In these lines, Symeon dissolves the schism between
body and spirit, mind and heart, this world and any other.

To *genuinely love Him* means to forget oneself and disappear
in that love. To become zero. Just twenty years before Sym-
eon was born, the great Sufi mystic Al Hallaj was crucified in
Baghdad by the Abbasid rulers for saying much the same as

his Christian brother would do thirty years later. For a year, Al Hallaj remained in silence and fasting, kneeling before the mosque in Mecca. Later, whenever anyone asked him what he saw and understood during that year, he would say "I am Truth, I am God. In my turban is wrapped nothing but God. There is nothing inside this cloak but God." This was not sweet music to the ears of the clerics, and the Abbasid rulers crucified him for "theological error."

Regarding Al Hallaj, Rumi said that

> people say it is presumptive to claim I am God, whereas it is an expression of great humility. The man who says "I am the slave of God" affirms two existences, his own and God's. But he that says "I am God" has made himself non existent and has given himself up and says "I am God, I am naught, He is all, there is no being but God's." This is the extreme of humility and self-abasement.[3]

In this self-forgetting,

> . . . *everything that is hurt, everything*
> *that seemed to us dark, harsh, shameful,*
> *maimed, ugly, irreparably*
> *damaged, is in Him transformed*
>
> *and recognized as whole, as lovely,* . . .

There is no part of us, no part of the living world, where He is not. When we see Him, we see Him everywhere. This is the meaning of the forgiveness of sins. We ourselves see that, the presence of God being everywhere; we are already forgiven in the depths of our own darkness, for He is already there. Absolution is a preexisting fact, awaiting our recognition of it through Him—not as a positive thought, nor as an adopted attitude, but as a falling away from our habitual identity into the unity that, to use the words of Symeon's faith, is Christ in and as all things.

Rumi put it this way:

> *"Lo, I am with you always," means when you*
> *   look for God,*
> *God is in the look of your eyes. . . .*[4]

That, in the words of Symeon, is to

> *. . . awaken as the Beloved*
> *in every last part of our body.*

10

ITHAKA

by C. P. Cavafy

As you set out for Ithaka
hope your road is a long one,
full of adventure, full of discovery.
Laistrygonians, Cyclops,
angry Poseidon—don't be afraid of them:
you'll never find things like that on your way
as long as you keep your thoughts raised high,
as long as a rare excitement
stirs your spirit and your body.
Laistrygonians, Cyclops,
wild Poseidon—you won't encounter them
unless you bring them along inside your soul,
unless your soul sets them up in front of you.

Hope your road is a long one.
May there be many summer mornings when,
with what pleasure, what joy,
you enter harbors you're seeing for the first time;
may you stop at Phoenician trading stations
to buy fine things,

mother of pearl and coral, amber and ebony,
sensual perfume of every kind—
as many sensual perfumes as you can;
and may you visit many Egyptian cities
to learn and go on learning from their scholars.

Keep Ithaka always in your mind.
Arriving there is what you are destined for.
But don't hurry the journey at all.
Better if it lasts for years,
so you're old by the time you reach the island,
wealthy with all you've gained on the way,
not expecting Ithaka to make you rich.

Ithaka gave you the marvelous journey.
Without her you would not have set out.
She has nothing left to give you now.
And if you find her poor, Ithaka won't have fooled you.
Wise as you will have become, so full of experience,
you'll have understood by then what these Ithakas mean.

drifting home

You might think that the man who wrote this poem would be an adventurer, a latter-day Odysseus who roams the world greeting everything before him with either the sharp end of his wit, his cunning, or his sword; the archetypal hero figure who always manages to survive the most implausible scrapes that would have anyone else tied in knots for decades or hung out to dry long ago. But no, C. P. Cavafy spent most of his adult life, some thirty years, toiling away as a clerk in the Irrigation Service of the Ministry of Public Works in Alexandria, Egypt. He was the shy, retiring man in the corner of the office, the one with the starched collar who went home every night to his mother's house and wrote fiercely passionate poetry. Not all that different a life story from another well-known poet, the Englishman Philip Larkin, who spent his years as a librarian in a humdrum northern town.

But Cavafy was from a radically different culture and world than Larkin's. He was born in Alexandria to Greek parents in 1863, the youngest of nine siblings. His family history was one of a comfortable and fashionable life, buoyed by the success of Cavafy Brothers, an import-export firm that came to fall on hard times when Cavafy was still young. Apart from seven years in London as a child, and some time in his family's native city of Istanbul, Cavafy lived out his life with modest means in the modest city of Alexandria, now only the most distant echo of the great city it once was under the Greeks and then Romans two thousand years before. Echo enough, however, to draw creative spirits like E. M. Forster, who served there with the Red Cross during the First World War, and later, in the forties, Lawrence Durrell and his coterie.

Both Forster's and Cavafy's works were inspired by the same two distinct passions: homosexual love and the ancient history of Greece in general and Alexandria in particular—"the phantom city that underlay the quotidian one," as Lawrence Durrell called it. While Forster wrote poetic history during his time in Egypt, including a guide to Alexandria, Cavafy wrote historical poetry as well as passionate love poems. After his mother died, Cavafy would often fantasize about living in a truly great city, a vital center of art and literature such as London, and would complain about the small corner of the world he found himself in. But he never moved from his source, and the city became his muse, hovering in the background and often the foreground of most of his poems.

He lived alone for twenty-five years, until his death in 1933, in the same second-floor apartment, which is now a museum honoring his life and work. At the time, it was in an old Greek quarter of the city. Nearby were a hospital, a church, and, below Cavafy's apartment, a brothel. "Where could I live better?" he once wrote. "Below, the brothel caters for the flesh. And there is the church which forgives sin. And there is the hospital where we die."

From this humble and ordinary life came the greatest poetry written in Greek during the twentieth century. Auden, among others, professed himself indebted to Cavafy's work and vision, with its uncompromisingly personal voice that managed to convey deep feeling at the same time as perspective, or distance, often through the use of irony. Not one volume of his poetry was made available for sale during Cavafy's lifetime, through his own choice. He would copy them and circulate them among friends, but was insistent on not confusing his art with money or reputation. Only after his death did a wider public begin to realize the greatness of this small man ensconced in a decaying city on the southern shores of the Mediterranean. The poem "Ithaka" was read at the funeral of Jackie Kennedy Onassis, and is delivered frequently at graduation ceremonies around the United States today. "The God Abandons Antony" is the source and inspiration for Leonard Cohen's song "Say Goodbye to Alexandra Leaving" on his album *Ten New Songs*. Like so many other great artists, Cavafy's reputation sprang to life only after his death, and has been growing ever since.

So here we have "Ithaka," the great journey poem that Cavafy composed as a significant variation on Homer's *Odyssey*, one of the first epic poems of Western literature. Throughout his ten-year journey home to his native island of Ithaka after the Trojan wars, Homer's hero, Odysseus, can think of nothing but of reuniting with his wife, Penelope, and his people. All the trials along the way are obstacles and troubles to be overcome as soon as possible, for the goal of arriving is the only thought in our hero's mind. Cavafy's narrator, however, urges the reader to

> *hope your road is a long one,*
> *full of adventure, full of discovery.*

We, then, are Odysseus. We are the hero on our way home. But Cavafy encourages us not to rush, not to fill our minds with nostalgia for the homecoming, as Odysseus did. Over the course of the poem, we come to see that the real meaning of Ithaka is the journey it inspired in the first place.

Both Dante and Tennyson before Cavafy also diverged from Homer's original theme, but with a different conclusion and also a different perspective on human nature. They both described an Odysseus who, on arriving home after a long absence, soon tired of what his homeland had to offer him, and set out again for new adventures and new lands. Cavafy, however, assures us (his hero and reader) that arriving in Ithaka is indeed what we are destined for, that you should

> *Keep Ithaka always in your mind.*

The force of destiny was intrinsic to the ancient Greek worldview; it was central to Homer's story, in which all the adventures, the troubles, and happy ending of Odysseus's journey were foretold from the beginning. Cavafy, Greek to the core, retains the same sense of destiny here. The end of our journey is always there, even from the beginning, and even if we can't quite put it into words. Not only death, which is everyone's end, but also the particular and personal way in which our own story reaches its conclusion—all this is unavoidable, however much we may try to fight and argue with the inevitable. Throughout his poetry, he tells us to face our life for what it is, without illusions. Everything that happens along the way is also part of Ithaka, the destination, and happens in the only way it can. As I mentioned in the first essay in this book, this is the message in his poem "The God Abandons Antony," where he tells Antony to stand there and watch as his god and protector, Dionysus, with all his beauty and music, leaves him—a sign that Alexandria, the city he has come to love, must leave him too.

So as we set out on our life voyage, we need have no fear of monsters as long as we keep our *thoughts raised high*, which means, Edmund Keeley suggests in his fine introduction to *The Essential Cavafy,* that we keep our mind and attention on what is in front of us, in the form of the present adventure or shape our life is taking in this moment, rather than worrying about where it is all taking us, how we might end up, or whether we will ever get where we want to go or not. The excitement of the present undertaking is what will keep our spirits free of

> *Laistrygonians, Cyclops,*
> *angry Poseidon—don't be afraid of them . . .*

The Laistrygonians were the giant inhabitants of an island that Odysseus and his crew landed on during their voyage.

When the giants saw them, they pelted them and their ships with boulders the size of men, sinking every ship but the one Odysseus captained. The Greek hero managed, of course, to escape, but the majority of his men were smashed to pieces or speared like fish. Cyclops was the one-eyed monster who, on the island of Sicily, shut all the Greeks in a cave with himself and his sheep, rolling a great boulder across the entrance. Every now and then he would snatch up a sailor for breakfast.

Telling the Cyclops that his name was Nobody, Odysseus managed to trick him into drinking himself drunk over dinner. The Greeks seized the opportunity to drive a huge stake into the Cyclops's only eye. When the monster cried out in pain for help from the other Cyclops on the island, and they asked who had harmed him, he called out "Nobody." So of course, nobody came to his rescue. Eventually, the Cyclops needed to let his sheep out, and the Greeks each clung to the underbelly of a sheep. Wily, Odysseus was. But the story was not over yet: The Cyclops happened to be the son of the old man of the sea, the god Poseidon, so he called upon him to make waves, which he duly did, causing Odysseus yet more delay and setbacks.

None of this need befall us, Cavafy says, unless we already carry the seeds of such tribulations within us already. External events, then, are only the reflection of internal forces at play within ourselves. Yet surely we all carry such seeds, and not necessarily just out of fear and anxiety for the future. We do this because trouble is part of the human drama. Perhaps we do this because dysfunction operates more or less in everyone's genes, certainly because the trouble we create, as when Odysseus blinded the Cyclops, tends to bring more storms from other, unexpected directions, even if only much later on in our story.

Trouble may come, but it is not what happens that matters, or even where we go, so much as how we respond to each turn in the road as it comes. Cavafy's poem asks us to adopt an attitude of curiosity and interest, if not joy, in whatever island our life brings us to, especially those islands, those experiences, that we are encountering for the first time. But more than that, he asks us to seek out those ports of call that might not seem on our most direct route home, that offer us new forms of beauty and pleasure,

> *mother of pearl and coral, amber and ebony,*
> *sensual perfume of every kind . . .*

And new forms of knowledge, such as may have been found in ancient Egypt in Odysseus's time. Homer's Odysseus never went to Egypt, or to Phoenicia (in the region of present-day Syria and Lebanon); he attempted to return from Troy directly to Ithaka, a small Greek island in the Ionian Sea, north of the Peloponnese, though he didn't reckon with Poseidon, the Sirens, the Cyclops, and all the rest. Cavafy doesn't want us to rush for the goal as Odysseus did, whatever it is we may think our goal is. He wants us to linger in foreign ports, to nourish both our senses and our mind to the full. He wants us to experience worlds and peoples that are not our own, because we are not here for long and only once.

I sometimes feel like this in America. I live here, I speak roughly the same language, yet this country remains faintly foreign, even so. I don't know if I will be here until I die. After all, I am inescapably European, with a different sensibility, with different landscapes and different cadences etched in my brain. Yet I love this corner of Marin County, beyond the Golden Gate Bridge, its people, its ocean, its beauty, its glorious bay. I am in no hurry to leave it, though I can sense that, for all its attraction, it may be an especially beautiful "island" on the way, the way to Ithaka, wherever and whatever that is. At the same time, from a deeper perspective, all the islands—the people and the places that we linger with— are part of our Ithaka. The journey itself is the destination, though the mystery (of a human life) will always make Ithaka far more than the sum of its parts.

Cavafy tells us in this poem to enjoy our journey, wherever it takes us, and to let it take as long as it takes; and the more exotic, the more outside of our habitual parameters it takes us, the better. Yet

> *Keep Ithaka always in your mind.*
> *Arriving there is what you are destined for.*

What do you think he means by this? Perhaps for you Ithaka means God, or Truth, or the final fulfillment of a lifelong dream. Yes, it means homecoming, of course, but the point, I think, is to hold the question in mind, to let it shimmer there, rather than jump to a ready answer. What matters, Cavafy says, is that you become rich along the way, so that your hopes do not rest on some final pot of gold at the end of some imaginary rainbow, some dream of paradise where all the conditions are exactly as you would like—the perfect relationship, the perfect home, the ultimate spiritual realization. The richness of Ithaka is that it gives us the journey, and that is all she has to give.

> *And if you find her poor, Ithaka won't have fooled you.*
> *Wise as you will have become, so full of experience,*
> *you'll have understood by then what these Ithakas mean.*

We will have understood through the living of it all, through the immersion—the fuller the better—in the places and people our lives present us with along the way. And in Cavafy's view, the more our senses and our minds are nourished in this way, the more our spirit can come to rest in its true home, the more we shall have come to understand what Ithaka means.

about the poets

ELLEN BASS (b. 1947)

Billy Collins has said of Ellen Bass's work that her "frighteningly personal poems about sex, love, birth, motherhood, and aging are kept from mere confession by the graces of wit, an observant eye, an empathetic heart, and just the right image deployed at the right time." Bass is the author of several nonfiction books, including *The Courage to Heal,* which has been translated into nine languages. Her poetry volume *Mules of Love* (BOA, 2002), won the Lambda Literary Award, and she has also won the Pushcart Prize and the Pablo Neruda Prize for poetry. Her most recent collection, *The Human Line,* came out with Copper Canyon Press in 2007. Bass teaches in the low-residency MFA Program at Pacific University, and has taught poetry and creative writing in Santa Cruz, California.

CONSTANTINE P. CAVAFY (1863–1933)

Cavafy was the most original and influential Greek poet of the twentieth century, though close to a third of his poems were never printed in any form until after his death. He was born in Alexandria, Egypt, and his family moved to England for seven years when he was nine; from there they went to Istanbul for two years before returning to a life of genteel poverty in Alexandria. Cavafy, who was homosexual, lived with his mother until

her death in 1899, then with his unmarried brothers, and fi-
nally by himself. He worked for thirty years as a government
clerk in the Ministry of Public Works in Egypt. He had a twenty-
year acquaintance with the English writer E. M. Forster.

LEONARD COHEN (b. 1934)

Leonard Cohen was born in Montreal, Canada. His artistic ca-
reer began in 1956 with the publication of his first book of
poetry, *Let Us Compare Mythologies*, which was reissued by Ecco
in a fiftieth-anniversary edition. Cohen is the author of twelve
books, including two novels—*The Favorite Game* and *Beautiful
Losers*—and the recent collection of poems and songs *Stranger
Music*. He has made seventeen albums, of which *Dear Heather* is
the latest. His haunting songs have left their mark on a genera-
tion who came of age in the sixties and seventies. Internation-
ally celebrated for both his writing and his music, Cohen is one
of the great legendary performers and artists of our time. His
Book of Longing, finally completed after his time as a monk in
Mt. Baldy Zen Center, outside Los Angeles, is an inspired col-
lection of poetry and line drawings.

JACK GILBERT (b. 1925)

Jack Gilbert, born in Pittsburgh, was educated both in his home-
town and in San Francisco. Soon after publishing his first book
of poems, *Views of Jeopardy*, in 1962, he went on a Guggenheim
Fellowship to Europe, where he stayed for many years, mostly in
Greece. *Monolithos*, his second volume, was published twenty
years after his first. Gilbert has always remained firm in his
avoidance of the beaten path to success and recognition, pre-
ferring the authenticity of a life on a remote Greek island to the
ambitions of New York City. The poet James Dickey once said,
"He takes himself away to a place more inward than is safe to go;

from that awful silence and tightening, he returns to us poems of savage compassion." Gilbert's *Refusing Heaven,* published in 2005, won the National Book Critics Circle Award. His latest collection, *Transgressions: Selected Poems,* was published by Blood-axe Books in 2006. Gilbert lives in western Massachussetts.

HAFIZ (c. 1320–1389)

Goethe was one of the first Westerners to discover Hafiz (sometimes spelled Hafez), whom he considered "a poet for poets." Ralph Waldo Emerson discovered Hafiz through Goethe's work, and did several translations of his own into English. The complete collection of his poems, the *Diwan-i-Hafiz,* still sells more copies today in his native Persia (Iran) than any other book. Hafiz was born and lived in the city of Shiraz. Of lowly stock, he worked as a baker's assistant by day and put himself through school at night. Over many years he mastered the subjects of a classical medieval education, which included the great Persian poets. In medieval Persia, poetry was valued very highly, and during his middle years, Hafiz served as a court poet. By the time he was sixty, he had become famous for his inspired verses, and he became both a spiritual and literary teacher for a wide circle of students. He was guided by a great Sufi master for most of his life, and he in his turn became a master for others in his later years.

JANE HIRSHFIELD (b. 1953)

Hirshfield is a prize-winning poet, translator, editor, and author of six collections of poetry. Born in New York City, she received her BA at Princeton University in the first graduating class to include women. She went to San Francisco and was a full-time practitioner at the Zen Center there for many years. Her collection *Given Sugar, Given Salt* was a finalist for the National Book

Critics Circle Award in 2001. Her work addresses the life of the passions, the way the objects and events of everyday life are informed by deeper wisdoms and by the darkness and losses of life. Her poetry searches continually for the point where new knowledge of the world and self may appear, and carries the influence of her lifelong study and practice of Buddhism. Her most recent collection is *After,* published by HarperCollins in 2006. She lives in the Bay Area.

MARIE HOWE (b. 1950)

The poet Stanley Kunitz said Howe's "long, deep-breathing lines address the mysteries of flesh and spirit, in terms accessible only to a woman who is very much of our time and yet still in touch with the sacred." Marie Howe's poems have appeared in the *New Yorker,* the *Atlantic Monthly, Harvard Review,* and *New England Review,* among other publications. She is the author of three collections of poetry, the most recent of which is *The Kingdom of the Living,* published by W. W. Norton in 2008. Hers is a poetry of intimacy, witness, honesty, and relation. She teaches at Sarah Lawrence College in Bronxville, New York.

RAINER MARIA RILKE (c. 1875–1926)

Rilke survived a lonely and unhappy childhood in Prague to publish his first volume of poetry, *Leben und Lieder,* in 1894. In 1896 he left Prague for the University of Munich. He later made his first trip to Italy, then Russia. In 1902 in Paris he became friend and secretary to the sculptor Rodin, and the next twelve years in Paris saw his greatest poetic activity. In 1919 he moved to Switzerland, where he wrote his last two works, *Sonnets to Orpheus* and *Duino Elegies,* in 1923. He died in Switzerland, of leukemia, in 1926. His reputation has grown enormously since his death, and he is now considered one of the greatest poets of the twentieth century.

ST. SYMEON THE THEOLOGIAN (c. 949–1022)

St. Symeon is one of the most beloved of saints in the Christian Orthodox Church. He is one of only three great Fathers who have been granted the title of Theologian by the Church, because he is one of a very few in the history of Christianity who is considered to have "known God." Theology, in the Orthodox tradition, is considered to spring from direct revelation rather than from study and learning. St. Symeon's whole teaching was of the availability of a personal experience of the living Christ. His writings, which are easily available today, grew out of his preachings and spiritual directions to the monks who were in his charge. He is still eagerly read by Orthodox monks, and is finding an increasing audience in Roman monasteries, too.

DAVID WHYTE (b. 1955)

David Whyte was born and raised in the north of England, studied marine zoology in Wales, and trained as a naturalist in the Galápagos Islands. He has led anthropological and natural history expeditions, and also runs occasional poetry and mythology trips to Ireland. He now lives in the Pacific Northwest with his wife and two children, and works full-time as a poet, reading and lecturing throughout the world. He is one of the few poets to bring their insights to bear on organizational life, working with corporations at home and abroad. He has published five volumes of poetry, and has also written two best-selling works of nonfiction, *The Heart Aroused: Poetry and the Preservation of the Soul in Corporate America* (Doubleday) and *Crossing the Unknown Sea: Work as a Pilgrimage of Identity* (Riverhead).

notes

INTRODUCTION

1. Jane Hirshfield, private interview with author.
2. John Keats, in a letter to John Taylor, February 1818, from *Keats: Poems and Selected Letters,* ed. Carlos Baker (New York: Scribner's, 1962).
3. Saul Bellow, quoted in Azar Nafisi, *Reading Lolita in Tehran* (New York: Random House, 2003).

1. SONNETS TO ORPHEUS, PART TWO, XII

1. Rainer Maria Rilke, "Archaic Torso of Apollo," *Poems of Rainer Maria Rilke,* trans. Robert Bly (San Francisco: Harper-SanFrancisco, 1981).
2. C. P. Cavafy, "The God Abandons Antony," *C. P. Cavafy: Collected Poems,* trans. Edmund Keeley and Philip Sherrard (Princeton, N.J.: Princeton University Press, 1992).
3. T. S. Eliot, *The Four Quartets* (New York: Harcourt Brace, 1988).

2. GATE C22

1. Ellen Bass, "Jack Gottlieb's in Love," *Mules of Love* (Rochester, N.Y.: BOA Editions, 2002).
2. Ellen Bass, "Sometimes, After Making Love," *ibid.*
3. Anna Swir, "The Greatest Love," trans. Czesław Miłosz and

Leonard Nathan, *Talking to My Body* (Port Townsend, Wash.: Copper Canyon Press, 1996).

3. EACH MOMENT A WHITE BULL STEPS SHINING INTO THE WORLD

1. Naomi Shihab Nye, "Kindness," *Words Under the Words: Selected Poems by Naomi Shihab Nye* (Portland, Ore.: Far Corner Books, 1995).
2. Rhonda Byrne, ed. *The Secret* (New York: Atria Books, 2006).
3. Rumi, "Love Dogs," *The Essential Rumi,* trans. Coleman Barks (San Francisco: HarperSanFrancisco, 1997).

4. LEAVING MT. BALDY

1. Leonard Cohen, *Beautiful Losers* (New York: Vintage, 1966).
2. Irving Layton, quoted on Leonardcohen.com.
3. Leonard Cohen, "Early Morning at Mt. Baldy," *The Book of Longing* (New York: HarperCollins, 2006).
4. Leonard Cohen, "Pardon Me," *ibid.*
5. Leonard Cohen, "Anything Which Refers," *ibid.*
6. Leonard Cohen, "When I Drink," *ibid.*
7. Leonard Cohen, "Early Questions," *ibid.*
8. Leonard Cohen, "Titles," *ibid.*
9. Leonard Cohen, "What Do You Really Remember," *ibid.*
10. Leonard Cohen, "What Did It," *ibid.*
11. Rumi, *The Essential Rumi,* trans. Coleman Barks (San Francisco: HarperSanFrancisco, 1997).

5. WHAT THE LIVING DO

1. Marie Howe, "The Last Time," *What the Living Do* (New York: Norton, 1997).
2. Marie Howe, "The Gate," *ibid.*

3. Rainer Maria Rilke, "Sunset," *Selected Poems of Rainer Maria Rilke,* trans. Robert Bly (New York: Harper Row, 1981).

4. Ellery Akers, "Advice from an Angel," *Knocking on the Earth* (Middletown, Conn.: Wesleyan University Press, 1988).

5. Rainer Maria Rilke, "Ninth Duino Elegy," *Duino Elegies,* trans. David Young (New York: Norton, 2006).

6. Leonard Cohen, "Anthem," *The Future* (Sony, 1992).

6. A BRIEF FOR THE DEFENSE

1. Nazim Hikmet, "It's This Way," *Poems of Nazim Hikmet* (New York: Persea Books, 2002).

2. Naomi Shihab Nye, "Kindness," *Words Under the Words: Selected Poems by Naomi Shihab Nye* (Portland, Ore.: Far Corner Books, 1995).

3. Wendell Berry, "Why," *Given* (Emeryville, Calif.: Shoemaker & Hoard, 2006).

4. W. H. Auden, "Musée des Beaux Arts," *Collected Poems of W. H. Auden* (New York: Modern Library, 2007).

5. Rainer Maria Rilke, "Sonnets to Orpheus, VII," *Selected Poems of Rainer Maria Rilke,* trans. Robert Bly (New York: Harper Row, 1981).

6. T. S. Eliot, *The Four Quartets* (New York: Harcourt Brace, 1988).

7. C. P. Cavafy, "Things Ended," *C. P. Cavafy: Collected Poems,* trans. Edmund Keeley and Philip Sherrard (Princeton, N.J.: Princeton University Press, 1992).

7. WHAT TO REMEMBER WHEN WAKING

1. Mary Oliver, "The Summer Day," *New and Selected Poems,* vol. 1 (Boston: Beacon Press, 2005).

8. WITH THAT MOON LANGUAGE

1. Jacob Needleman, *Why Can't We Be Good?* (New York: Jeremy P. Tarcher/Putnam, 2007).
2. St. Paul, Romans 7:19.

9. AWAKEN AS THE BELOVED

1. St. Symeon, "The Three Methods of Prayer," *The Philokalia,* vol. IV, compiled by St. Nikidimos of the Holy Mountain and St. Makarios of Corinth, trans. G. E. Palmer and Philip Sherrard (New York: Faber & Faber, 1995).
2. Evagrius, quoted by Abbot John Bamberger, Abbey of the Genesee, New York, in his address there on November 3, 2002.
3. Rumi, quoted in the entry on Al Hallaj on Wikipedia.com.
4. Rumi, *ibid.*

acknowledgments

My gratitude goes first of all to the ten poets whose work in this book has been an inspiration to me. Then to Kristin Bowers, delightful dancing partner, who first suggested that I should give Ten Poems a new birth in this way. To Patricia, for being such an intimate presence in my life during the time of writing. To my dear friend Amy Gross, for the impassioned discussions we had over many a lunch on the themes in the essay on "White Bulls." To dearest Lama Palden, deep friend for all time, with whom I have explored these topics for years, as I have too with Jennifer Welwood. To Faisal Muqaddam, spiritual friend. To John Prendergast, for his valuable comments on the St. Symeon essay. To John Haule, for his brilliant work *Divine Madness: Archetypes of Romantic Love*, and to my dear friend of many years Jacob Needleman, for his wonderful book *Why Can't We Be Good?* Joy Harris, indefatigable agent, and Shaye Areheart, editor, publisher, loyal friend, I am always and ever grateful for your continuing support and belief in my work. Thank you.

permissions

about the author

ROGER HOUSDEN remains English, although he lives in Marin County over the Golden Gate Bridge from San Francisco. He loves the weather there, the people, the mountains, and the ocean. But then he also loves Italy. You can reach him through his website at roger@rogerhousden.com.